MW00978959

Best wishes,

Out Of The Shadows

American Women Who Changed The World

Anna Nevenic

RAVE PUBLISHING

Out Of The Shadows

Library of Congress Cataloging-in Publication Data has been applied for.

ISBN 0-9747508-0-8

ACKNOWLEDGMENTS

I would like to thank Preeti Aroon who helped in the writing and researching and my editor Lionel Rolfe.

I am also grateful for all the women throughout American history who were brave enough to take a stand and swim against the currents of the times in order to advance the causes of peace and justice in our world. I am almost indebted to all the writers and researchers who documented those struggles. Without them, there indeed would be nothing about which to write.

Last, I thank the authors of the books and Web sites used to compile all the information presented in this book. The content of this book rests upon the shoulders of all who have done diligent research and preserved the memories of these women in books and other publications.

—Anna Nevenic
Los Angeles, CA
October 30, 2003

Contents

INTRODUCTION

TODAY WE HEAR OVER and over again from individuals of all walks of life who say the world is out of control. No one person can make it better. But from my reading, I long ago developed an optimistic view of human nature. History is often made by just one percent of its individuals. Enough mistakes have been made in the past, we should be able to learn what mistakes not to keep repeating.

All societies have great stories to tell, stories that can inspire their members to get involved and make a difference. Just as America has produced many great heroes and heroines, so do people in other parts of the world. But I think that America has affected the whole world and this era in so many ways.

The end of the 19th century brought excess of riches for America's elite. The early, most pre Civil War Industrial Revolution, produced a small number of wealthy individuals. But by the time of World War I, it was not elected officials who were in control of the government. It was corporate America, which ruled the country almost unencumbered by laws and regulations. Unsafe food, electoral fraud, poverty, child labor, and exploitation in general, prevailed over everything. The existence of a civil society was very much threatened.

A handful of courageous individuals saw the problems and decided to dedicate their lives and expertise to solving them. Some of these courageous individuals were men and some were women, however this book is about women—the most courageous women of the nineteenth and twentieth centuries who actually changed the face of America. With tremendous commitment and energy, these women improved the quality of life for many and brought dignity to the majority of the American people.

Journalists who dared to report the truth of unscrupulous corporations and such were known as "muckrakers." The term has stuck around for a long time. Jessica Mitford, for example, never minded the nickname she earned for her books, "Queen of the Muckrakers."

The first and earliest of women rebels who attacked the system of the past were the suffragists. These women were on fire as they pursued the right of women to vote and to control their own destinies. The suffragist message affected not just America, of course. Many countries were split by the suffragists. Those first women activists were reviled in their towns, churches, and social clubs, and in the streets they were treated like common criminals. They endured ridicule, contempt, and arrest, but they never gave up the fight until they had won.

This book is not necessarily for scholars, seeking a sophisticated and in-depth analysis of how American women advanced the cause of peace and justice. Rather, this book is intended for "everyday" people who may not even have had much exposure to American history beyond what they learned in high school (if they have completed high school at all).

Rather, this book intends to provide a general overview of the development of feminism in the United States. It also provides concise biographies of the key women in the United States who demanded peace and justice. The intent of these biographies is twofold. The first intent is to give readers an understanding of how these remarkable and brave women came to embrace the cause of peace and justice. The second intent is to provide the reader with an appreciation of these women and the reforms that they enacted. The United States would not be the great country it is today without these women.

WOMEN WITH NO HISTORY

THE SUBORDINATION OF WOMEN began with hunter-gatherers settling down to farm the land. Men took over agriculture and animal care, which prior to this were considered women's jobs. With this new division of labor, men achieved greater authority outside the home. On the other hand this new division of labor placed women inside the house for the first time. This new family order established patriarchal society, placing men at the head of the household and giving them absolute authority over its content, including the women and children.

Patriarchy was firmly planted as early as 3000 BCE. In some ancient civilizations, women had greater privileges and rights and in some they had no rights at all. Egyptian women received great favors that were in large part due to the civilization's tradition of goddess worship. Women were given freedom to participate in some of the same rites and ceremonies as men.

Patriarchy is actually an institutionalized male supremacy that started somewhere in Mesopotamia in the Middle East over 24,000 years ago, and this belief in the system of patriarchy gradually spread across the globe. There were many insurgencies and revolutions that have challenged ruling classes. However, feminism is the first movement that challenged patriarchy itself. Today, in every country, women are organizing and demanding to be treated as human beings.

Interestingly enough, it was in Greece, the so-called Cradle of modern Democracy, where patriarchy was carried further than anywhere else. There was no area in which Greek women had any rights. Greek women held virtually no status in ancient Greek civilization. Women in Athens were treated as minors and were under guardianship of a male during their entire lives. Greek women living outside of Athens fared a little better. In Sparta girls were allowed to train for athletic events and even to study with boys.

During the sixteen, seventeenth and eighteenth centuries, many social changes around the world took place simultaneously. The Renaissance, which began near the end of the Middle Ages, brought the rebirth of Western civilization. These centuries and the events that they brought planted the first seeds of the social and political development of the modern world.

For centuries women were excluded by law and by custom from active participation in affairs of state and affairs of family. Indeed, before more modern times, the few women who were strong leaders were the exceptions and not the norm. This exclusion of women in political affairs began to change in the beginning of the 20th century when women around the world began to demand the right to vote. It took over 100 years for women in the United States to achieve this right, and by the end of the twentieth century women in nearly every country had won this political victory.

Throughout history there have always been a handful of women who challenged the view of the world around them. These women were not afraid to speak out about injustice. Usually, however, these were women of a higher social status, which afforded them greater freedom to do what they wanted to do with their lives. By the seventeenth and eighteenth centuries the number of women questioning the status quo and defying society's inequalities and mores had greatly increased.

Discovery of the New World—North and South America—brought new change for the old. European immigration to the New World brought expanded economic and personal opportunities for both genders. Male colonists needed all the people they could get, and they demonstrated their appreciation to women colonists by giving them almost equal footing in the newfound countries. However although these women had some economic rights, their legal rights did not change in the New World. Just like the English common-law, the women were expected to relinquish all their personal property and rights to men once they got married.

But as the colonies developed, the rights enjoyed by the earliest female settlers were eroding. They were no longer given equal land grants. Women in American colonies fought side by side with men during the American Revolution. Although they fought together with men to gain freedom for their country, their own status and rights did not improve very much after the Revolution.

The nineteenth century brought profound changes in literally all phases of life in the U.S. and the effects of these economic and social changes were unprecedented. The U.S. of the nineteenth century promised unlimited opportunities, yet its people faced many problems working out the standards by which they would conduct themselves.

Defining women's role in society became a fundamental quest for nineteenth century social and political arenas. This period became obsessed in its quest for prescribing and regulating the proper role of women. An ideology for controlling the lives of women and their behavior was created, and it was known as the "Appropriate Sphere of Women." This newly created women's sphere was one of subordination to men, a way of life to which most women adapted and even believed to be the natural order of things.

Still, between 1750 and 1850 the circumstances of women's life changed economically and socially. Agricultural families functioned as economic units and the tasks of both husband and wife were essential. Both worked at home and, although divisions of labor were made between the genders, most functions were overlapping.

The Industrialization Period (1800–1860) brought changes for women as well, expanding occupational opportunities in some fields outside the domestic circle. Some single women gained a measure of independence from their work in the factories. However this personal independence didn't mean a break from restrictive home environments. The girls who worked in mill towns were treated as the mill's property on the job as well as off the job. Their employers supervised the young women's conduct and their lives in boarding homes as well as their religious behavior.

Nineteenth century theories on femininity emphasized a division in U.S. culture where men and women were assigned contrasting roles. Men were portrayed as aggressive, physical, and unchaste, and women as pure, selfless, dedicated, and domestic. Thousands of essays and articles were urging women to help civilize the nation. And many middle class women answered these calls. Clergymen made no secret of enlisting women to revive the interest in religion and church. Women were especially responsible for running Protestant religious institutions.

The interpreters of the "Women's Appropriate Sphere" emphasized female morality and a woman's role as guardian of the nation's purity. The thinking was that it was the women's duty to protect their families from evil. Post-revolutionary thinkers and theorists agreed that American women had serious responsibilities as mothers in maintaining the moral values of the young people. These same theorists saw that those responsibilities could be fully realized only through women's education. Therefore, for these reasons, the education of women was regarded as appropriate. The educational reformers advocated the best educational instructions for women so that they can raise great sons. Girls' schools, on the other hand, in the early nineteenth century included science, but still expected the emphasis from female teachers to be religious and moral training for their offspring.

Emma Willard was the founder of one of the earliest seminaries for women in New England. Willard argued against discrimination in education based on sex; however, she was not a feminist and she never asked for emancipation of women in other fields. She accepted the common notion of her time that women's subordination was permissible because it was divinely ordained. Willard's school curriculum was superior to other schools because it included algebra, geometry, history, geography and a variety of science courses. She was a great supporter of women teachers, training hundreds of them in private and public school settings. It is estimated that more than 200 schools used Willard's method of education.

The seminary movement of the 1850s demonstrated the teaching abilities of women, and most of the seminary promoters campaigned to make teaching a major vocation for women. There was a great shortage of teachers and the supply of qualified men was shrinking while at the same time an increasing number of women was emerging from seminaries and academies, filling up the educational cup. The answer to the teacher shortage was to employ these educated women, and, of course, it didn't hurt that women teachers were paid poorly compared to men.

At first there was a resistance to women in the classrooms, but the resistance gradually broke down once the men in power saw the economic advantage of hiring women over men. It became evident that women were willing to teach for less money; most other professions were closed to them and teaching was the only way educated women had to utilize their skills.

Still, educational opportunity paved the way for middle class women to organize the women's movement.

Simultaneously, the missionary movement was expanding drastically after the 1800s and female societies were also emerging simultaneously.

The connection of women and religion had particularly strong support in cities and small towns. In addition to supporting religious causes, many women's societies provided assistance to the poor and the sick. Women in the benevolent societies served as the right hand for the clergy. These women's organizations were efficient in raising money not only for their religious causes but also for other social poverty relief efforts. The benevolent women's societies were a stepping-stone for the emergence of women reformers and social workers such as Dorothea Dix, Clara Barton and Jane Addams. The path of women's "social feminism" was also developing, and this movement can be considered as direct descendants from the organized religious benevolent societies.

Many women's labor organizations developed in the industrialization period after the 1830s. Women were becoming deeply involved in the industrial revolution's labor movement. They tried to set minimum wage standards and campaigns were organized seeking a ten-hour working day in the factories. These early women activists saw themselves as revolutionary mothers trying to assert their rights as "free women."

But by the 1840s, women were running into lots of opposition—and that kept them from developing strong bonds in the Labor movement, mainly because of the opposition or indifference of men. The capitalist structure in textile mills and other industries opposed any collective action by women workers. In the patriarchal atmosphere of early nineteenth century industrialism, mill owners had almost total power over their workers. The collective engagement of women in religious benevolent societies and seminaries complimented the efforts of male leaders. On the other hand, collective labor movement threatened the authority and the economic power of corporate male leaders.

THE RELIGIOUS WAR
AGAINST WOMEN

IN EVERY COUNTRY BARRIERS were created to keep women down in political and economic systems. But in more recent times—primarily in the last four decades—with the rise of the international women's movement, improvements have been made in the lives of women in the workplace.

But there are institutions around the world that are working to revoke the gains that women have made, and these major institutions are religious.

Most of the major world religions are patriarchal by their nature. Under pressure from feminism, a number of churches are trying to eliminate the most obvious patriarchal elements from their teachings. On the other hand many churches are becoming fanatically patriarchal again and are responsible for the creation of a rigid movement called fundamentalism. Although some fundamentalist groups do not share any religious principles, these groups are all equally promoting a fanatic male control over women.

The fundamentalists of the Christian faith drew their inspiration from the belief that the Bible was dictated by God. That makes the Bible the highest authority. Christian fundamentalists generally are very militant. They

19

are ready to fight for their religion, whether by attacking modernist theology or secular affairs of the state. It can be said that fundamentalists are religious warriors who share their combative nature with their Muslim and Jewish counterparts.

The heart of fundamentalism is based not only on an abstract belief about the Bible; rather, prescribed life behavior is at the core of their beliefs. They forbid any sexual behavior outside marriage and even prohibit any verbal reference to sexuality. They are very adamant about extending their contradictory beliefs to the entire society.

Fundamentalists are usually subservient to their charismatic male leaders and strongly oppose the involvement of women in what they regard as the in the "male sphere." The family is the primary focus and the assumption is that women should take on only the roles of their so-called "natural state" that revolves around the family.

Fundamentalism first appealed to men who were living through the great social changes that occurred between 1880 and 1930 (particularly after World War I). The expansion of the great consumer economy was a part of this. The period after World War I affected Americans in every aspect of their lives. The period also brought the most intense changes in the sex roles and attitudes as well.

The men who dominated fundamentalism felt threatened because they felt they were losing control over "their" women. After the 1860s, more young women were allowed decent educational opportunities, a newfound freedom that created new job possibilities outside the home. As many of these women were able to gain their own economic and social resources, their fathers felt they were losing control of their daughters. In addition women gained certain powers within marriage as laws were passed guaranteeing married women property rights.

The first wave of suffragettes fought for the basic rights of women—the right to own property and to get an education. As contraception was illegal, suffragettes created a voluntary motherhood movement. These motherhood organizations supported women who were controlling the frequency of sex within marriage in order to avoid unwanted pregnancies. For the first time women were asserting control over their own bodies. The voluntary motherhood movement was the first step in preventing rape and other sexual abuses of women within the marriage.

Many women for the first time were able to reclaim control of their own bodies and many educated women postponed marriages and many refused to marry at all. Married women were divorcing at an unprecedented level. Between the 1870s and 1930s the United States divorce rate more than quadrupled.

By the turn of the twentieth century, women had gained some degree of independence. At the same time, fundamentalists became obsessed with domestic relations and sexual behavior. They felt that marriage was under attack by feminists. Many preachers seemed more concerned about the behavior of women than issues of religious principles.

The fundamentalist literature of the 1920s called for a return to Victorian ideology. Fundamentalist journals spoke openly about how God had designed woman as the homemaker. The fundamentalists chastised women who were pursuing their career goals and blamed them for losing track of their natural place in the family. To fundamentalists, the emancipation of women was equal to the destruction of the family. These religious advocates believed they were saving the family. They also thought that women had made religion "too soft," and for that reason the churches should be returned to male control. In their view, men should be in authority in all spheres of life because that is the law of nature. Women's role primarily belongs within the domestic sphere. Christian fundamentalists portrayed women suffragettes as unnatural, responsible for destroying the true nature of womanhood and family structure. Up to this point in American life mostly women attended churches and very few men did. In order to attract men to attend the church services, the fundamentalist zealots made sure that women would not be allowed to speak as authorities in the church any longer. The fundamentalists—men, mostly—believed that church has become feminized and too compassionate and in order to attract men they advocated that the church must become more masculine by emphasizing virility, militarism and heroism.

Fundamentalist journals opposed ordaining women to traditional parish ministry, even if women were practically running the churches during the nineteenth century since men had abandoned the church in large numbers during this period. Twentieth century fundamentalists became very intolerant of any female leadership in churches.

Fundamentalists praised everything about militarism, militant tactics, and inflexibility. They opposed so-called modernist theologies. Women who held power in church and were college professors were referred to as "effeminate ginks." A thorough analysis of fundamentalism clearly suggests that the movement rose up primarily to counter feminism and to reassert male control in society.

The changes in family power structure were seen as a threat to the social order of things, changes that the fundamentalists attributed to a loss of faith and the lack of genuine belief in the true Bible. To fundamentalists, the cure for everything was to be found in the Bible.

Fundamentalists also opposed teaching the theory of evolution because they said it would destroy morality and human responsibility. They saw the world through sexual and gender-oriented eyes. Morality related mostly to female behavior—female crime was equated with divorce and young women drinking and smoking.

Today's fundamentalist opposition to abortion and divorce is nothing new. Those ideas are as old as fundamentalism itself. These new fundamentalists have become extremely vocal over the past three decades, and in their political activities are anxious to tear down the separation of church and state. They are extremely anti-feminist and homophobic. They sense that these things threaten their dominance.

They have made alliances with men like Reagan and both the Bushes and other conservative politicians. They are rigidly opposed to compromise and accommodation with any other belief.

They justify their involvement in political activism because they want to make society conform to their own moral values. Out of this movement evolved Jerry Falwell and his Moral Majority, a special interest group with millions of followers. These followers want to impose their views on the rest of American society and government.

WOMEN REFORMISTS

TODAY, IN MOST INDUSTRIAL countries, many women are educated and most women are allowed to work in a variety of fields. However, in non industrial and developing nations, the process have been slow for women to get and hold political power.

Even in developed countries, the small minority of women who hold political office and who are in the public realm are subjected to many personal attacks and unwarranted criticism of a kind rarely directed at men. The intensity of the dislike for women in the public arena has even extended to the wives of political leaders. Barbara Bush was the only First Lady to escape criticism because publicly she never demonstrated any influence over her husband's political life. The criticism of women and personal attacks against them have functioned as a constant reminder that female leaders are under constant surveillance by men.

The patriarchal system that operated for centuries in order to legitimize male superiority omitted women from all kinds of history. Few people were aware of the many accomplishments of women who were rulers, scientists, artists, writers, and inventors. Many women were leaders of early unions, but once unions became a political force, this changed.

During the 1830s American women took part in a series of reform movements that aimed to humanize American society. Questions under discussion included war, education, the improvement of prisons, and, most importantly, the issue of slavery.

The nineteenth century reformist efforts had two tones—one was secular and the other religious. Secular reformers drew their principles from the philosophies of the Enlightenment. The United States was established with ideals that came from the Enlightenment. Reformist idea of the Enlightenment deeply affected women who were involved in religious benevolent societies. Women were not just asking to improve human conditions through charities; the reformists were speaking and writing about changing governmental institutions. Women who sought social change were primarily focused on the specific problems that came out of the experience of being women. Thus the movement for moral and social reforms and anti-slavery agitation appealed to women because they too were the victims of the system which they were attacking,

In addition to the anti-slavery and the temperance movement, women were involved in educating young black girls during the first part of the nineteenth century. Prudence Crandall organized her own school in Connect-icut and recruited seventeen black children from New England states. Prudence was threatened and eventually jailed on the basis of a so-called law against "harboring vagrants." Her conviction was secured because the judge told the jury that blacks were not citizens of the United States, even if they were free and lived in a free state.

Throughout all the trials and turbulence, Prudence kept her school open, but physical violence eventually shut it down. The windows of the school were broken; manure was dropped in the water well; and local storekeepers refused to sell food to the school. For a year and a half, Crandall and her supporters held their ground and kept the school open. Not until the school was fire bombed did she accept the agonizing defeat.

It was women who initiated a boycott of cotton and other products made by slave labor. The use of petitions was a form of protest used by women even in the Victorian era. Because of their personal exposure in public places women were able to circulate petitions among friends in private homes as well as at church and other public events. These anti-slavery women were able to recruit thousands of supporters to their cause.

For eight years, Congressional leaders refused to accept any petition from anti-slavery women. South Carolina Senator Pickney introduced a Gag rule into the Senate that specifically prohibited the submission of anti-slavery petitions in Congress. The battle was finally won under the presidency of John Quincy Adams and the American people established for the first time their right to petition government to hear people's grievances.

Abolitionists won the argument that slavery was a matter of federal policy and not a matter for the state to decide individually. Soon, to help make the abolitionist points, women developed oratorical skills and literary eloquence. The writings and speeches of such courageous and remarkable women as Lucy Stone, Lydia Maria Child, Sara Parker, Anna Dickinson, Susan B. Anthony, Sojourner Truth, Harriet Beecher Stowe, and others, meant tens of thousands of people were being reached which helped to provide a strong opposition to the prevailing pro slavery policy.

The publication of Harriet Beecher Stowe's novel *Uncle Tom's Cabin* in 1851 was a critical event in the history of the anti-slavery movement. Without doubt, this piece of work caused public outrage and attention on an unprecedented scale. *Uncle Tom's Cabin* sold over 300,000 copies in the United States and more than five times that in England. The book was translated as well into many other languages

THE GRIMKE SISTERS, PIONEERS OF THE ABOLITIONIST MOVEMENT

THE TWO WOMEN MOST instrumental in the abolitionist movement were Angelina and Sarah Grimke. The sisters were raised by a well-to-do slave holding family in South Carolina. They abhorred slavery and left home to avoid witnessing its cruelties. Compelled by their moral beliefs, they publicly denounced the system they knew so well. Because they knew the system so well, the Grimke sisters became two of the most effective organizers in the service of the anti-slavery movement.

Angelina became one of the abolitionist movement's greatest public speakers and she was the first woman ever to address a legislative body in Massachusetts. On February 21, 1838, Angelina Grimke presented the members of the legislative committee with a petition with 20,000 signatures, demanding the immediate abolition of slavery. Her anti-slavery crusade was based on egalitarian principles evoking moral and religious condemnation against the perpetrators of slavery. Angelina insisted that blacks have a natural right to freedom. To her, slavery in whatever form represented a violation of the natural order of things.

APHRA BEHN: THE FIRST WOMAN TO SPEAK AND WRITE HER MIND

APHRA BEHN DESERVES PARTICULAR recognition, for she was the first woman who gained for women the right to speak their minds. Aphra was the first English woman to become a professional writer. She successfully forced the men who dominated the circle of letters in seventeenth century England to recognize her as an equal. She demonstrated that a woman, if willing to surrender respectability and comfort and if prepared to risk ridicule, might be able to declare her autonomy and make a living by writing in an age where usually one's social status and economical survival depended solely on marrying a wealthy man.

Women participated in the reformist movement of the 1830s by becoming the dominant force in the temperance and peace movements. As a direct result of promoting world peace, two organizations were formed, the Women's Christian Temperance Union in the 1870s and the Women's International League for Peace and Freedom in the beginning of the twentieth century. Although advocacy for peace did not have the mass appeal of the women's temperance movement, the movement did attract a significant group of women, most notably Quaker women.

The apex of women's involvement with reformist ideals came with the anti-slavery movement. American abolitionists drew inspiration from the British movement for total emancipation of slaves. Women joined the anti-slavery movement from the moment of its inception. Just as women were attracted to moral reforms, they recognized the need for action against the morality of slavery. Elisabeth Margaret Chandler joined forces with Benjamin Lundy, a Quaker. Margaret Chandler was a regular correspondent for *Lundy's* journal where she appealed to women to organize anti-slavery societies.

By the late 1830s, thousands of American women played a role in their own anti-slavery societies. Later, men and women worked together on the abolishment of slavery. The Philadelphia Female Anti-Slavery Society was one of the most influential of these groups. This group had such prominent members as Sarah Angelina Grimke and Lucretia Mott. These women carried on the group's daily activities in addition to visiting black families and providing them with daily necessities. At this time they were distributing anti-slavery periodicals and articles all over the state.

Women's fairs were the major fund-raising projects for the anti-slavery movement. These fairs provided many opportunities for women to meet and discuss the major issues of the anti-slavery cause. The fair system brought together anti-slavery societies from different regions, and put them in a place where they could exchange ideas and develop a sense of community.

Women's anti-slavery agitation served as a preamble to the equal rights movement. The slavery issue raised more questions about the status of women than benevolent societies had. The anti-slavery movement was about the issue of human rights and freedom, the same principles that applied to the condition of women.

The women's rights movement became more intense after the Seneca Falls Conference in 1848. The basic aim of feminists at the time was to achieve human rights for women. Justice was what women sought the most—and justice involved getting the legal rights that would enable women to control their own property. The feminist human rights agenda was based on the principle of equality, not superiority or subordination. The argument for justice applied to economic, moral, and political rights.

Feminists wanted autonomy and the right to decide for themselves how to live their lives. They wanted women to be recognized as full human beings by allowing them to define their own so-called "sphere of life."

The struggle for women's rights became an engine for change, demanding the end of restrictions and challenging conventional male attitudes. The early feminists of the seventeenth and eighteenth centuries started a struggle for equality and autonomy for all women and this struggle has continued to the present day.

The achievements of feminist movement are nothing less than a revolution, and the ideals and the accomplishments of its pioneers cannot be forgotten nor taken for granted.

THE FIRST WAVE OF FEMINISM

ABIGAIL ADAMS (1744–1818), wife of John Adams (the second president of the United States), sowed many of the seeds that would later get Americans, both women and men, to reconsider the status of women in a country that in principle was dedicated to equality and freedom.

As was common for children of that era, Abigail received no formal education. In Abigail's time, girls at most were taught reading and writing so they could read the Bible and write letters. They also were taught basic arithmetic to prepare them for their future roles as housewives, when they would have to balance budgets and settle accounts.

Abigail, however, was lucky to have a father, William Smith, who loved learning and reading. In fact, he encouraged all his children, including Abigail, to share in his passion. He gave Abigail and her siblings complete access to his extensive library of books. Abigail grew to share her father's love of books and read widely in subjects including poetry, drama, history, theology, and political theory. Over the years, Abigail became increasingly determined to educate herself, and by the time she was an adult, she had become one of the best-read women of her time.

Nevertheless, the gaps in Abigail's education bothered her and the crudeness of her literacy was apparent in her letters. Her spelling was poor and inconsistent. She was ashamed of her inability to use punctuation properly as well as of her poor handwriting. In spite of these obstacles, however, Abigail remained determined in her quest to educate herself and further develop her mind.

One should not take lightly Abigail's passionate efforts to educate herself. As a woman, she was taking both a unique and brave stance in her determination to swim against the currents of her time when she sought to educate herself. One must remember that the primary aim of eighteenth century women was to get married and raise a family. Education was mostly seen as an endeavor that played no legitimate role in a woman's life. In fact, women even feared becoming too educated, for they believed that potential grooms would pass up young women who were "too clever" in favor of those who were more lighthearted and flirtatious.

After Abigail married John Adams, she soon became pregnant and found herself embedded in what would become a familiar pattern in their marriage. She remained at home and managed the vast responsibilities of an eighteenth century household (overseeing servants, handling accounts, and stocking and preparing food), while John traveled to Boston and other nearby communities pursuing his career as a lawyer.

With cases in Boston, and other parts of New England, he spent weeks and months away from home. Although she abhorred these long absences, she felt it was a wife's duty to support her husband in all he aspired to and did not want to prevent him from reaching his highest potential.

With the stirrings of the American Revolution, John Adams was elected a delegate to the first Continental

Congress in Philadelphia. This duty took him even further away from his family and for longer times as well.

With John in Philadelphia, Abigail entered a new period in her married and personal life. She had an increased responsibility of managing a large household without her husband. Using her adept mind, she ensured that the operations of the house and farm ran smoothly, economically, and efficiently. Her success in running the affairs of the home provided her with an increased sense of confidence and assurance in her abilities as a woman. This confidence was demonstrated when she even took it upon herself to make some investment decisions. After several years of managing a large household, Abigail began to refer to the house and property as "my own affairs," rather than "ours." She no longer referred to these affairs in her letters to John as "your affairs."

One must keep in mind that in Abigail's time, women had few choices in deciding the direction their lives would take. A female's life was clearly mapped out from childhood to old age; as girls, females received little formal education. Any education received had only to be sufficient enough to enable them to manage their duties as housewives. Rather than pursue formal education, girls and women were directed to take up what were considered more feminine pastimes, such as sewing, music, letter writing, and being a hostess. Once women were married, they were expected to serve as helpmates to their husbands and create a harmonious and peaceful home to which their husbands could happily return at the end of a weary day.

Abigail recognized that women had little freedom to determine the direction their lives would take, and for the most part she accepted that reality. What made her unique for her time, however, was that she insisted that a woman's role carried an equal amount of importance and responsibility as a man's. Abigail saw herself as fully contributing to the success of her husband when he became vice president and then president of the United States. She had supported her husband through every step of his career. While he was away for weeks and months at a time, she put up with years of loneliness, raised a family, and single-handedly managed a large and busy household. She never interfered when career duties demanded his time, even if this meant being separated from him for long periods. Thus, it was only a natural consequence that she believed that women, whose role was equally as important as that of men, were entitled to the educational opportunities and legal and political rights that would enable them to achieve their fullest capacity within the domestic sphere which society had prescribed to them. She wrote, "Let each planet shine in their own orbit, God and nature designed it so. If man is Lord, woman is Lordess ... if a woman does not hold the Reigns of Government, I see no reason for her not judging how they are conducted."

Denied a formal education, Abigail was a self-taught woman who placed enormous value on developing her mind, challenging her thinking, and continuing to learn. When she lived in England during the late 1780s, she even sought to educate herself in science, an area which few woman dared, or were even permitted, to go. She signed up for a series of twelve lectures about such subjects as electricity, magnetism, hydrostatics, optics, and pneumatics. She attended five of those lectures. The experience inspired her and gave her a heightened appreciation for the vast world of ideas from which women were shut out. In remembering the science lectures, she wrote,

"It was like going into a Beautiful country, which I never saw before. A Country which our American Females are not permitted to visit or inspect." Thus, Abigail's unflagging insistence on education for women stemmed from the totality of such life experiences.

Throughout her life, Abigail was plagued by the frustration that she had been denied the opportunity to receive the same classic education given to males of her era. She fervently affirmed that education was as equally important for women as for men, and she made sure that her own daughter received a good education. In many of Abigail's letters, to both women and to men, she wrote passionately of her conviction for girls' and women's education. In a letter to her husband, she wrote: "You need not be told how much female education is neglected, nor how fashionable it has been to ridicule Female learning." Abigail averred that a woman could more competently perform her required duties in the domestic sphere, including child rearing, household management, and "retaining the affections of a man of understanding" if she were given a proper formal education. She wholeheartedly agreed with her friend Mercy Otis Warren who said that, since women were responsible for the early education of their children, they must themselves be educated so that they could adequately meet this responsibility.

As an aside, it should also be noted that Abigail's advocacy for the expansion of freedom and education was not limited to just women. A visit below the Mason-Dixon line reaffirmed Abigail's conviction that slavery was not only evil, but also a threat to the development of America's nascent democracy. On March 31, 1776, Abigail wrote that she doubted the leaders of the colony of Virginia, a slave holding state, had quite the "passion for Liberty" they claimed to have, considering that they had been used to "depriving their fellow Creatures" of freedom.

On February 13, 1791, she wrote to John about a black servant boy who had asked her about going to school to learn to write. Abigail enrolled him in a local evening school. A neighbor reported the serious objections of several people to the boy's presence. Abigail promptly responded that the boy was "a Freeman as much as any of the young Men and merely because his Face is Black, is he to be denied instruction? How is he to be qualified to procure a livelihood? ... I have not thought it any disgrace to my self to take him into my parlor and teach him both to read and write." No further complaints were made.

Abigail's dedication to expanding educational opportunities for women in particular, however, was so passionate that she urged her husband to include the issue into the laws that he and the other founding fathers were drafting in 1776. With a hopeful spirit she wished "that our new constitution may be distinguished for learning and Virtue ... If we mean to have Heroes, Statesmen, and philosophers, we should have learned women." Surprisingly, her husband John wrote back that he was in exact agreement with Abigail's views on this subject!

When it came to the general independence of women, however, John was not always in agreement with her. In 1776, while John and the other Congressmen were in Philadelphia drafting the laws to guarantee independence for the colonies, Abigail made her most passionate plea for women's rights. She wrote to John appealing to him to remember that women also needed to be given the right to independence.

Her letter to John reveals an eerily prophetic sense of women's struggles to come, as well as an insightful understanding of the danger of making one group subject to the will of another: "I long to hear that you have declared an independency and by the way in the new Code of Laws which I suppose it will be necessary for you to make I desire you would Remember the Ladies, and be more generous and favorable to them than your ancestors. Do not put such unlimited power into the hands of the Husbands. Remember all Men would be tyrants if they could. If particular care and attention is not paid to the Ladies we are determined to foment a Rebellion, and will not hold ourselves bound by any Laws in which we have no voice, or Representation."

John did not take Abigail's passionate plea very seriously at first. He wrote back in a mocking tone: "As to your extraordinary Code of Laws, I cannot but laugh. We have been told that our Struggle has loosened the bands of Government everywhere. That Children and Apprentices were disobedient ... that schools and Colleges were grown turbulent ... that Indians slighted their Guardians and Negroes grew insolent to their Masters. But your Letter was the first Intimation that another Tribe [women] more numerous and powerful than all the rest were grown discontented. This is rather too coarse a Compliment but you are so saucy, I won't blot it out."

Not easily discouraged, Abigail shared her radical views with her friend Mercy Otis Warren, and even spoke of petitioning Congress to consider her views. Although she never did so, her proposal did have some effect. John seemed to have taken her ideas a bit more seriously and to have given her views considerable thought as he struggled with the issue of voters' rights. He understood that a government built on the principles of freedom and equality and carried out with the consent of the people must by reason include women in that equation. With foresight, he wrote to Brigadier General Joseph Palmer on the issue of suffrage, "Depend on it, Sir, it is dangerous to open so fruitful a source of Controversy and altercation, as would be opened by attempting to alter the Qualifications of Voters. There will be no end to it. New claims will arise. Women will demand a vote."

Interestingly, it would be almost 150 years later, in 1920, when John Adam's insights on freedom and equality would come true, and women would be granted the right to vote.

Despite her unflagging determination to promote educational opportunity and legal rights for women, Abigail ended up bringing about no immediate changes in the way women were treated or perceived. Nonetheless, she was undoubtedly ahead of her time and distinguished herself as being among the first women in the new country to seriously consider a woman's rights and role in a free society. It would not be long before other women of like mind followed her lead and began working to bring about real and lasting change. In essence, Abigail had planted the seeds of what would grow to be a true revolution in women's rights and opportunities.

Sources

Information in the previous chapter was obtained, paraphrased, and quoted from:

http://www.galegroup.com/free_resources/whm/bio/
adams_a.htm

http://www.galegroup.com/free_resources/whm/bio/
adams_a.htm

http://www.umkc.edu/imc/adamsa.htm

http://www.umkc.edu/imc/adamsa.htm

http://www.uua.org/uuhs/duub/articles/abigailadams.html

JANE ADDAMS:
AN EARLY FEMINIST

JANE ADDAMS (HER FIRST name was actually Laura) was a one of the first generation of privileged American women who obtained a college education and then dedicated their lives to community service and social justice. Born in 1860, she lived until 1935, enough time to have seen a lot of women's history.

Jane saw the westward expansion of the U.S. government; the industrial revolution; the progressive era of political reform; and the Protestant ethic of hard work, intellectual achievement, and duty to serve others. She was an American social reformer who established the model for all immigrant settlement houses, providing social services, including education and childcare, to the poor. She won worldwide recognition in the first third of the twentieth century as a pioneer social worker in America, and also recognition as a feminist and an internationalist.

In 1931, Jane became the first American woman to receive the Nobel Peace Prize.

Having come from a comfortable, middle class background, Jane did not have to "work to survive" or "earn a living." Most other women coming from her type of background accepted a life in a "good marriage" and settled into a pattern of homemaking, church activities, and relatively limited participation in philanthropic causes.

Jane was different, however, and she chose to make use of her college education in a way that would challenge her intellectually and spiritually. Jane was of the firm conviction that she had been educated to serve, and she wanted to serve in a way that would have a true impact on the lives of people who had not been fortunate to have the same advantages as she had.

After the completion of her education, Jane traveled to Europe twice. At the age of twenty-seven, during her second tour to Europe with her friend Ellen G. Starr, she visited a settlement house, Toynbee Hall, in London's East End. There, she first encountered the concept of a "settlement house" and observed well-educated university graduates living in a community of working class and poor people. These settlement workers organized clubs, recreation, and educational programs for people in the neighborhood. The distinguishing characteristic of the settlement was its ability to deliver services without employing professional social workers or welfare agency staff who were often judgmental and punitive in the way they treated poor people.

This visit to Toynbee Hall settlement house finalized Jane's idea of opening a similar house in an underprivileged area of Chicago. In 1889, she and Ellen leased a large home built by Charles Hull at the corner of Halsted and Polk streets. The two friends moved in with the objective "to provide a center for a higher civic and social life; to institute and maintain educational and philanthropic enterprises and to investigate and improve the conditions in the industrial districts of Chicago."

Jane and Ellen made speeches about the needs of the disadvantaged neighborhood, fundraised, convinced young women of financially comfortable families to assist, cared for children, nursed the sick, and listened to outpourings from troubled people. By its second year of existence, Hull House provided assistance to two thousand people weekly. Kindergarten classes took place in the morning; club meetings for older children were provided in the afternoon; and in the evening, more clubs or courses were available for adults in what became essentially a night school. The first facility added to Hull House was an art gallery. The second was a public kitchen. Afterwards there came a coffee house, a gymnasium, a swimming pool, a cooperative boarding club for girls, a book bindery, an art studio, a music school, a drama group, a circulating library, an employment bureau, and a labor museum.

At the time the Hull House was founded, the westside of Chicago was characteristic of the large, northern, industrial urban areas of nineteenth century America. As a center of industry and commerce, Chicago served as a gateway between the manufacturing northeast and the agricultural midwest. After the civil war, the U.S. expansion westward to claim new territories gave impetus to an incredible burst of growth in transportation, manufacturing, and commerce. This economic expansion required cheap labor, and therefore the U.S. government encouraged massive migrations from Europe. The Halsted street neighborhood where Jane Addams made her home was a typical slum complete with overcrowded tenements, crime, disease, inadequate schools, inferior hospitals, and insufficient sanitation.

The abundance of non-English speaking new Americans who had come predominantly from southern and

Eastern Europe overwhelmed the public welfare agencies, mutual aid societies, and municipal government. Newspapers from that time teemed with reports and editorials expressing the fears of "foreigners, anarchists, and unwashed rabble" who had no knowledge of American democracy and who supposedly had no contribution to make to American culture. The public was greatly concerned as to how quickly the new arrivals would give up their old ways, and assimilate into mainstream America. The prevailing belief at the time was that until immigrants gave up their language, customs, and loyalty to the old countries, they were a threat to American political, economic, and social structures.

Not surprisingly, immigrants saw themselves quite differently from the way the mainstream press did. Many immigrants had arrived with little more than the clothes on their backs and their heads filled with tales of "streets of gold." While the merchants and factory owners of the busy and bustling city of Chicago were eager to hire immigrants, most were unwilling to pay a decent wage or accept any responsibility for creating the conditions which perpetuated the slums. Moneyed interests easily corrupted local politicians, and city services (such as garbage removal, building safety codes, and police and fire protection) were disturbingly inadequate.

The prevailing economic conditions required parents to work long hour. Consequently, small children were left unsupervised and older children were forced to fend for themselves. Education was inadequate, and teachers untrained to deal with ethnic diversity in a sensitive manner and were scornful of children who could not speak English. Recreational facilities were non-existent and as a result, juvenile delinquency, prostitution, and petty street crime became serious threats to the safety of everyone in the tenements.

Forced to work in appalling conditions, disdained by the community leaders who exploited their labor but ignored their needs, the immigrants of Chicago's westside were without hope or means of escape.

It was here that Jane brought herself, her political ideals, and her conviction to live by a certain set of principles. She was a student and an advocate of the progressive political movement, which espoused such ideas as political reform, women's suffrage, pacifism, cultural pluralism, dignity of labor, social justice, rights of children, the need for public health and safety rules, and the duty of government to protect the vulnerable. She believed that civic, religious, and philanthropic organizations needed to join into partnership with community residents and government to solve the problems that created slums. Jane believed that immigrants would enrich American culture if given ample opportunity to participate in it.

Thus, Jane established her residency in Hull House based upon several basic principles.

First, Jane wished to live in the community as an equal participant in the local issues of the day. Unlike the social workers and society matrons who visited the poor and then returned to their middle class homes every evening, Jane and her colleagues lived where they worked. The "settlement" concept was central to the success of the Hull House community, and the practice of "neighbors helping neighbors" became a cornerstone of the Hull House philosophy.

Second, the Hull House community believed in the fundamental dignity of all individuals and accorded every person whom they encountered with equal respect while learning about their ethnic origins, cultures, and customs.

Third, the Hull House community believed that poverty and the lack of opportunity bred the problems plaguing the slums. Ignorance, disease, and crime were the result of economic desperation and not the result of some moral flaw in the character of the new immigrants. Jane promoted the idea that if afforded a decent education, adequate living conditions, and reliable income, any person could overcome the obstacles posed by the slums.

Additionally, an inhabitant of the slums, if allowed to develop his or her skills, could not only make a better life for himself or herself, but could also contribute to the community as a whole, she believed. Access to opportunity was the key to successful participation in a democratic, self-governing society. The greatest challenge and achievement of the settlement was to "help people help themselves."

Implementing these principles was no small task. Jane had to gather around her a community of young men and women, all well educated and willing to sacrifice personal comfort, to risk living in a hostile community, and to experiment actively in seeking solutions to the challenge of slum life at the turn of the century. The activities of Hull House included citizenship and literacy classes; adult education; sports and hobby clubs; theater and dance programs; cooking, sewing, and homemaking classes; public baths; day care; health clinic; visiting nurses; immunization programs; art appreciation; libraries; political discussion groups; lectures on educational and workplace reforms; and meeting spaces for labor meetings, mutual aid societies, and social clubs. Most importantly, Hull House created a forum for public debate on policy and legislative issues in municipal, state, and national arenas.

The achievements of the Hull House community were numerous and its impact was incalculable. This group of idealistic young women and men made Hull House the most famous settlement house in the U.S. and generated ideas, proposals, and policy reforms still felt a hundred years later. Civil rights, women's suffrage, international peace, juvenile protection, labor relations, court reform, public health, public housing, civic watchdog, and urban planning movements can all trace their origins, at least in part, to the work of the Hull House settlement.

As her reputation grew, Jane was drawn into larger fields of civic responsibility. She played an important role in many local and national organizations. She was a founder of the Chicago Federation of Settlements in 1894 and she also helped to establish the National Federation of Settlements and Neighborhood Centers in 1911.

In 1905, she had been appointed to Chicago's Board of Education and later made chairwoman of the School Management Committee. In 1908, she participated in the founding of the Chicago School of Civics and Philanthropy and in the next year became the first woman president of the National Conference of Charities and Corrections (later the National Conference of Social Work). She was a leader in the Consumers League. She was chair of the Labor Committee of the General Federation of Women's Clubs, vice-president of the Campfire Girls, and a member of the executive boards of the National Playground Association and the National Child Labor Committee. In addition, she actively supported the campaign for women's suffrage and the founding of the National Association for the Advancement of Colored People (1909) and the American Civil Liberties Union (1920).

In Chicago, she led investigations on midwifery, narcotics consumption, milk supplies, and sanitary conditions. Jane even went so far as to accept the official post of garbage inspector of the Nineteenth Ward, at an annual salary of a thousand dollars. In 1910, she received the first honorary degree ever awarded to a woman by Yale University.

Jane wrote prolifically on topics related to Hull House activities. She wrote eleven books and numerous articles. Furthermore, she maintained an active speaking schedule nationwide and internationally.

Jane was a passionate feminist. In the days before women's suffrage, she staunchly believed that women should make their voices heard in legislation and therefore should have the right to vote. More broadly, she thought that women should form their own aspirations and search out opportunities to realize them.

In the early years of the twentieth century Jane became involved in the peace movement. To realize her aspiration to eliminate war from the world, she created opportunities or seized those offered to her to advance the anti-war cause. In 1906, she gave a course of lectures at the University of Wisconsin summer session which she published the next year as a book, *Newer Ideals of Peace*. With the publication of the book, Jane became publicly know as a pacifist. She spoke for peace in 1913 at a ceremony commemorating the building of the Peace Palace at The Hague and in the next two years, as a lecturer sponsored by the Carnegie Foundation, she spoke against America's entry into the First World War. For this public opposition to the war, Jane was attacked in the press and expelled from the Daughters of the American Revolution. She found, however, an outlet for her humanitarian drives as an assistant to Herbert Hoover in providing relief supplies of food to the women and children of the enemy nations, the story of which she told in her book *Peace and Bread in Time of War* (1922).

In January 1915, Jane accepted the chairmanship of the Women's Peace Party, an American political organization. Four months later she and other women from belligerent and neutral nations met at the International Congress of Women at The Hague in an attempt to stop the war. When this congress later founded the organization called the Women's International League for Peace and Freedom, Jane served as president until 1929, as presiding officer of its six international conferences in those years, and as honorary president for the remainder of her life.

After sustaining a heart attack in 1926, Jane never fully regained her health. Indeed, she was being admitted to a Baltimore hospital on the very day, December 10, 1931, that the Nobel Peace Prize was being awarded to her in Oslo. She was the first American woman to receive the prize. Jane died three days after an operation revealed unsuspected cancer.

By the time of her death, Jane had changed forever the profile of Chicago. By then, her reputation as the Mother of the World was firmly established. She had received letters from people around the world not only praising her for her inspirational work, but asking her to intervene on their behalf as they struggled against hunger, poverty, and oppression.

After Jane's death, the residents of Hull House carried on the work begun by Jane and the other founders. Hull House continued to serve the people of Halsted Street through the Depression of the 1930s and World War II. Seventy years after its founding, the original Hull House complex of thirteen buildings was sold to make way for the new campus of the University of Illinois, and Hull House moved to the northside of Chicago. After the move from Halsted Street, Hull House established two community centers: Jane Addams Center in Lakeview, and Uptown Center in a storefront on Wilson Avenue. In addition, other community centers located in southern, western, and suburban communities joined Hull House to become members of the modern Hull House Association.

Sources

Information in the previous chapter was obtained, paraphrased, and quoted from:

http://www.hullhouse.org/about.asp

http://www.swarthmore.edu/library/peace/Exhibits/ jane.addams/addams.index.htm

http://www.uic.edu/jaddams/hull/newdesign/ja.html

http://www.nobel.se/peace/laureates/1931/addams-bio.html

SUSAN B. ANTHONY, THE FIRST SUFFRAGIST

S USAN B. ANTHONY, WHO was born in 1820, became the New York State organizer for the abolitionist movement during the presidency of Abraham
Lincoln in the 1860s. However, Lincoln's Republican
platform promised only to prevent the expansion of
slavery while preserving the slave holding rights in the
states where it already existed. Anthony's slogan was
"No compromise with slave holders. Immediate and
unconditional emancipation."

Anthony toured New York State condemning slavery wherever she went. In all places where she gave her
speeches she confronted extreme violence from hostile
mobs. Her anti-slavery views and the views of her com-
patriots in the movement were far too advanced for this
particular moment in American history.

In addition to her anti-slavery work, she campaigned
tirelessly for legal reforms that would allow women
greater control over their own lives. In 1860, Anthony
and Elizabeth Cady-Stanton organized a women's rights
convention in Albany, New York, for passage of a property bill of rights. By 1862 the two women made a declaration that they would collect a million signatures in the

northern states in a petition demanding the immediate abolition of slavery.

This campaign for the abolition of slavery was conducted at the same time the riots against the military draft were spreading all over the New York state. For days, bands of white vigilantes attacked blacks, burned federal and state buildings, and violently attacked and killed anti-slavery supporters.

In the aftermath of this violence and unrest, women carried out their signature gathering campaign. Two thousand women were able to secure over 400,000 signatures within eighteen months. With their actions these women abolitionists displayed a sense of inter-racial solidarity and were able to develop class-consciousness. Collectively, these women were responsible for the passage of the 13th Amendment to the United States Constitution, which finally abolished slavery.

Even before the Civil War, a number of states had become testing grounds for black emancipation and women's rights. One measure endorsed ratification of the 15th amendment and the other provided women the right to vote in state elections. However, the Republican Party hierarchy, dominated by well to do industrialists and financiers, split its endorsement of the measures and voted down women's suffrage rights.

Susan B. Anthony and Cady-Stanton made a very wise decision to solicit support from the Democratic party leaders who were very happy to split the Republican Party even if it meant temporarily aligning themselves with women. Anthony and Stanton were not enthusiastic about a political alliance with a party of the former slaveholders, but they were willing to do anything in order to secure the suffrage for women.

The two women had learned through years of campaigning how to play a political game to their advantage. They traveled by train visiting wealthy Democratic leaders even if they were eccentric in their political views. The Democratic message favored women's suffrage on one hand and on the other hand was racist. In discussing the issues of women's suffrage, Stanton and Anthony kept silent on the issue of black suffrage.

One of the wealthy democratic leaders, a Mr. Train, even gave Stanton and Anthony money to publish their own newspapers. The first issue of the paper, *The Revolution*, came out in January of 1868. The Revolution addressed many issues related to the oppression of women including suffrage, education, divorce, domestic abuse, reproductive rights, and trade union organizing. The divorce question was a very sensitive and controversial topic in the nineteenth century because it directly attacked a man's property rights over his wife and children.

Stanton and Anthony opposed the 15th amendment. The two women proclaimed, "The Constitution shall know neither black nor white, neither male nor female, but only the equal rights of all classes. We renew our solemn indictment against this instrument as a defective, unworthy, and oppressive charter for the self-government of a free people."

A majority of the Equal Rights Association delegates voted to support the 15th amendment, and in protest Stanton and Anthony resigned their membership in the organization.

With the breakup of the Equal Rights Association, the unity of the two movements for black and female equality ended. Had this unity survived it was possible that the women and men of the Association would have be able to wage an effective defense for civil rights and women's rights simultaneously.

After the breakup of the Equal Rights Association, Anthony and Stanton searched for a progressive linkage, especially through the working class and the trade union movements. Although there were some obvious mistakes made over the battle for the 15th amendment, nevertheless it can be said that the women together and separately made a vital contribution to the abolition of slavery and the emancipation of women. Stanton was highly intellectual and through her writings and her speeches she was able to shed more light on the false male supremacist assumptions and theories on the family, sexuality, religion, and politics.

In all, the experience of these women has demonstrated that accomplishments can be achieved only through unity of different groups aiming for the same goal. Susan B. Anthony had significant relationships with African American women including Sojourner Truth, Ida B. Wells, and Mary Church Terrell. The abolitionist struggle that was undertaken by different groups set a new course in American history. Both black and white women had a vision that enabled them to fight together for their mutual freedom and political emancipation.

With the end of the Reconstruction Period in 1876 and the solid reaffirmation of white supremacist rule in the south, special state laws were passed to preserve segregation and to prevent black men from voting. By 1908—two years after Anthony's death—most of the states in the South had enacted constitutional provisions that provided for all of the southern states to have white primaries only.

By the beginning of the twentieth century, the repeal of the 15th amendment was under serious consideration. Certain arguments against some provisions of the 15th amendment were appearing not only in southern journals, but national periodicals as well. It was argued that although the 14th and 15th amendments granted blacks political rights, they did not provide for political equality. The opinion of some was that discrimination based on race was unconstitutional; however, the discrimination on the basis of literacy, ownership of property, and taxation was constitutional and moral. Even the U.S. Supreme court affirmed the constitutionality of these interpretations of the 15th amendment.

ELIZABETH CADY STANTON: SHE SET THE AGENDA

THE WORLD'S FIRST ORGANIZED movement for the benefit of women was inaugurated in July 1848, at a small chapel in the village of Seneca Falls, New York. In this historic event, thirty-two-year-old Elizabeth Cady Stanton delivered her first public speech. She was convinced that the time had come for the question of women's wrongs to be laid before the public. She strongly believed that women themselves must do this work, for only women alone could understand the depth and the intensity of their degradation. Elizabeth's positions on issues related to women, justice, and equality confirmed that women lived under a double standard which tolerated a high degree of freedom for males, but none for females.

Elizabeth was the driving force behind the 1848 Seneca Falls Convention, and for the next fifty years (she died in 1902) she played a significant leadership role in the women's rights movement. Somewhat overshadowed in popular memory by her long time colleague Susan B. Anthony, Elizabeth was for many years the architect and author of the movement's most important strategies and documents. Though she became increasingly estranged from the mainstream of the movement, particularly near the end of her career, she maintained to the end her long time friendship with Susan.

Born on November 12, 1815 in Johnstown, New York, Elizabeth was the daughter of Margaret Livingston and Daniel Cady, the town's most prominent citizens. In 1826, the death of her brother Eleazar drove her to excel in every area her brother had in an attempt to compensate her father for his loss. She received her formal education at the Johnstown Academy and at Emma Willard's progressive Troy Female Seminary, where she received the best education available for a young woman of the early 1830s. She also acquired a considerable informal legal education from her father, a prominent judge who trained many of New York's lawyers.

Early in her life, Elizabeth was introduced to the reform movements, including encounters with fugitive slaves at the home of her cousin Gerrit Smith. It was at Smith's home that she met her husband Henry Stanton, an anti-slavery orator. Through her marriage to him, Elizabeth was introduced to the most advanced circles of reform. Soon after their marriage in 1840 they traveled to London, where Henry was a delegate to the World Anti-Slavery Convention. There Elizabeth met Lucretia Mott, the Quaker teacher who served in many of the temperance, anti-slavery, and women's rights organizations with which Stanton was later associated. Denied her seat at the convention, as were all the women delegates, Lucretia discussed with Elizabeth the need for a convention on women's rights.

Elizabeth and Lucretia's plan came to fruition when, with three other women, Elizabeth spearheaded the first women's rights convention in Seneca Falls, New York, in July 1848. This first national women's rights convention initiated the women's rights movement in the United States and established Elizabeth as a leader of the movement. At this gathering, she presented the conference's Declaration of Rights and Sentiments, a document which she composed and modeled on the Declaration of Independence. The Declaration and its eleven resolutions demanded social and political equality for all women, including its most controversial and radical claim, the right to vote.

Elizabeth's arguments for woman's rights began where the American Revolution left off. Women were endowed with the same natural rights and rational minds as men. Therefore, as men's equals, women should be treated equally under the law and in political participation. From that starting point, Elizabeth also explored how true equality would transform interpersonal relations and pervasive cultural norms.

In 1851, Elizabeth met Susan B. Anthony while Susan was attending an anti-slavery meeting in Seneca Falls. Their remarkable friendship and collaboration began at once. History records the lasting relationship between these two women as well as the strains that resulted from their different roles and priorities. As a single woman, Susan was free to travel and earn her living from her reform work. Unwilling to commit to a vigorous travel schedule until her seven children were grown, Elizabeth managed during their childhoods to hone her gift as a writer, write many of her speeches to be delivered by Susan, and exert great influence over the antebellum woman's rights movement even though she rarely attended its meetings.

During the Civil War, Elizabeth and Susan formed the Women's Loyal National League, the first national women's political organization. Through the WLNL, 5,000 women gathered 400,000 signatures to persuade Congress to pass the 13th Amendment guaranteeing freedom for African Americans.

In 1866, Elizabeth and Susan helped establish the American Equal Rights Association, which was dedicated to securing suffrage for both African American men and all women. Though the two suffragists believed that women's suffrage could be enacted through the 14th, and later, the 15th Amendments, many of their abolitionist colleagues, including Gerrit Smith and Frederick Douglass, rejected the plan by arguing that votes for African American men must take precedence.

Feeling abandoned and betrayed over the subject of precedence, Elizabeth and Susan, along with Matilda Joslyn Gage, in May 1869 formed the National Woman Suffrage Association, a woman led organization devoted to obtaining a federal woman suffrage amendment. In retaliation, their estranged abolitionist colleagues formed the more conservative American Woman Suffrage Association in November 1869, a move which solidified the painful rupture in the woman suffrage movement.

During these dark days during the controversy over precedence from 1868 to 1870 Elizabeth and Susan published the radical women's rights newspaper *The Revolution*. Elizabeth was the principal writer and editor, and Susan was the publisher and business manager. Although the paper was a financial failure, it provided a much-needed forum for the two women to broadcast their views to their allies and the public.

After the Civil War, when Elizabeth felt free to travel, she became one of the best known women in the United

States. As president of the National Woman Suffrage Association, she was an outspoken social and political commentator who debated the major political and legal questions facing the U.S. As a witty and popular lecturer touring the nation, she spoke about issues such as maternity, the crusade against alcohol, child rearing, and divorce law, as well as constitutional questions and presidential campaigns. While she entertained her audiences, she challenged them to examine how inequality had distorted American society and asked them to think about how equality might be achieved.

The campaign for women's equality that was led by Elizabeth was received with ridicule from politicians, journalists and clergymen. She and her comrades met hostile audiences everywhere, but the women persevered in delivering speeches, circulating petitions, and making difficult journeys to towns and rural districts. They gave speeches to small groups in churches, city halls, or any place that was offered to them.

Almost thirty years after the Seneca Falls Convention, Elizabeth and Matilda Joslyn Gage authored the Declaration of Rights of the Women of the United States, which Susan presented, uninvited, at the country's centennial celebration in Washington, D.C. in 1876. The Declaration was signed in the Centennial Books of the National Woman Suffrage Association by Elizabeth, Susan, and Matilda, as well as by many later arrivals to the movement.

By the 1880s Elizabeth had tired of traveling and organizing women. At sixty-five years old, she became more sedentary and focused on her writing. With the collaboration of Susan and Matilda, she wrote the first three volumes of *A History of Woman Suffrage*, which covered the period from 1848 to 1877. In this work, published several decades before women had won the right to vote, the authors documented the individual and local activism that built and sustained a movement for woman suffrage.

Elizabeth was not exclusively a suffragist. Later in her career she focused increasingly on social reforms related to women's concerns. She was concerned with revolutionizing women's lives on many fronts through marriage and divorce reform, dress reform, expanded educational opportunities for women, and her protests against organized religion's oppression of women.

More specifically, Elizabeth returned to her lifelong examination of the relationship between organized religion and women's subordination. Along with scores of articles on the subject, she published her controversial biblical commentaries in *Woman's Bible*, the first volume of which was published in 1895. The *Woman's Bible* was the culmination of her life-long interest in correcting biblical passages that are demeaning to women. There she affirmed her own faith in a secular state and urged women to recognize how religious orthodoxy and masculine theology obstructed their chances to achieve self-sovereignty and become independent souls. The *Woman's Bible* became an immediate bestseller and aroused widespread controversy.

Elizabeth Cady Stanton died in 1902 and unfortunately did not live to see women's suffrage in the United States. She is nonetheless regarded as one of the nineteenth century's most prominent proponents and true major forces in the drive toward women's legal and social equality in the United States and throughout the world.

Sources:

The information in this chapter was obtained, quoted, and paraphrased from:

http://ecssba.rutgers.edu/studies/ecsbio.html

http://www.pbs.org/stantonanthony/resources/index.html?body=biography.html

http://www.nps.gov/wori/ecs.htm

SUSETTE LA FLESCHE TIBBLES: THE STRUGGLE FROM YET ANOTHER PERSPECTIVE

Susette La Flesche Tibbles, an Omaha Native American, campaigned tirelessly for Native American rights. She became the first Native American lecturer and the first published Native American artist and writer in the U.S. Born the daughter of Omahas Chief Joseph La Flesche in 1854, Susette studied at the Elizabeth Institute, a girl's school in New Jersey, and afterwards returned to her reservation to work as a teacher in a government school. Susette made her debut as an activist for Native Americans' rights soon after the Ponca Indians were forcibly removed from their lands in 1877. During the brutal displacement, more than a third of the tribe died and those remaining were relocated to unfamiliar territory. In the national uproar that followed, Susette traveled East in 1879 with newspaperman Thomas Tibbles of the Omaha *Herald* on a lecture tour designed to bring attention to the wrongs committed against the Ponca Indians. She garnered national attention by serving as translator for Ponca chief Standing Bear. Going by the English translation of her Native American name Inshta Theumba (*Bright Eyes*), Susette was able to inform influential easterners about the plight of the Native Americans. In 1882, she anonymously edited Standing Bear's book *Ploughed Under: The Story of an Indian Chief.*

She and Thomas Tibbles were married in 1881, and they continued to lecture in the U.S. and England on the rights of Native Americans to their own land. Their crusade led to the passage of the Dawes Act of 1887. At its time, the Act was considered to be a progressive law of benefit to the tribes. During the remainder of her life, Susette lectured occasionally, contributed regularly to various magazines and newspapers, and gained a minor reputation as an artist illustrator. She and her husband lived most of their years in Nebraska where she died on her native land in 1903.

Sources:

Information in the this chapter was obtained, quoted, and paraphrased from:

http://www.indigenouspeople.net/omaha.htm

http://www.greatwomen.org/women.php?action=viewone&id=97

http://www.greatwomen.org/women.php?action=viewone& id=97>

NELLIE BLY: A GREAT WOMAN JOURNALIST

NELLIE BLY WAS BORN in 1865 and from an early age she witnessed the cruelty of life. Everywhere she saw an unfair system where children were suffering, immigrants were living in poverty, and women were continuously struggling through life without even the minimum of basic rights. These images of injustice had a profound effect on Nellie and she decided early on that some day she would make a difference. She got her first chance to illustrate the face of injustice by writing about the plight of divorced women trying to gain full employment. Public reaction to her article was divisive. Some readers found this writing brilliant and some viewed it as indecent. But in spite of the disagreement among the public, her articles sold the papers. Many newspapers avoided the controversial issues for fear of offending the powerful, but in spite of everything Nellie used all her energy to write as many articles as she could.

Eventually, Nellie got a job at the New York *World*, the largest newspaper in the country. She promised the editor of the newspaper, Joseph Pulitzer, that she would write the most sensational story of the year. To achieve this goal, Nellie went undercover in the state asylum system. At the time the asylum system of the nineteenth century was a place where patients were treated even less humanely than animals. She wanted to expose the cruelty of the system, which she believed would shock the country. She faked a nervous breakdown and was publicly dragged off to the sanitarium for the insane. Nellie was shaken by what she saw in the asylum. Patients were beaten up, starved, and forced into the harshest labor. Her story, "Behind Asylum Bars" was, as she had predicted, an immediate sensation. The story was picked up by papers all across the nation, and Nellie became the most famous journalist in the country. Because of Nellie's amazing investigative reporting skills, the conditions in New York's asylums for the mentally ill were greatly improved. Throughout her life, Nellie continued to write about the causes and issues that touched her conscience and her heart. The government often disliked her stories and eventually she was shunned because of her truthful reporting.

MOTHER JONES: THE GREATEST REBEL THERE EVER WAS

MOTHER JONES (BORN MARY Harris Jones in 1830, she lived a full century) grew up in Ireland, where her grandfather was hanged for his involvement with the Irish liberation movement, which sought independence from Great Britain. In 1838, when Mother Jones was still a child, her father fled Ireland because he had the same beliefs as his father.

After high school, Mother Jones worked as a teacher in Michigan before moving to Memphis, Tennessee. There, she married George Jones, an iron molder. It was from her husband that she learned much about unions and the psychology of workingmen. Tragically, Mother Jones' husband and four children died within one week in 1867 due to a yellow fever epidemic.

After losing her family, she relocated to Chicago, where she worked as a seamstress. Her biographer Dale Fetherling believes that Mother Jones' interest in the labor movement really began here, where she saw the stark economic inequalities between the wealthy families for whom she worked and the poor people living in the slums. According to Fetherling, Mother Jones said: "Often while sewing for the lords and barons who lived in magnificent houses on the Lake Shore Drive, I would look out of the plate glass windows and see the poor, shivering wretches, jobless and hungry, walking alongside the frozen lake front. The contrast of their condition with that of the tropical comfort of the people for whom I sewed was painful to me. My employers seemed neither to notice or to care."

Tragedy struck Mother Jones once again when she lost all her belongings in the 1871 Chicago Fire. This tragedy was a pivotal moment in her life and afterwards she started to follow a new path in life. She became involved with the Knights of Labor and the labor movement. She made Chicago her home base while criss-crossing the country fighting injustice. When asked where she lived, she answered, "Wherever there is a fight."

Mother Jones participated in most of the strikes that engulfed the United States during the late 1800s. Regardless of the difficulty of the situation, she was able almost single-handedly to keep a strike alive for a long time. The union members admired her talent as a strike organizer and the strikebreaking companies despised her.

Her talent as a strike organizer was unmatched by no other. She was able to organize the spouses of the strikers and without the support of these women, there would have been no chance that the strikes could have survived. Mother Jones instructed the women to bring their babies with them to the strike site and during their arrest women would sing all night. They also would allow their babies to cry during the night. These actions drove the jailers crazy, and consequently the women would be released from the jail.

In addition to union work, Mother Jones also fought for the rights of children who were exploited in factories during the day, working side by side with their parents. She led a movement in Philadelphia against the abuse of children who were working in the textile industry and factories. Mother Jones reiterated the theme in many of her speeches, "Philadelphia's mansions were built on the broken bones, the quivering hearts and drooping heads of these children."

Even in her nineties, Mother Jones was fighting for the rights of steel, garment and streetcar workers. Her last known public speech was in 1926 when she was the guest of honor at a Labor Day celebration in Alliance, Ohio. Her last public appearance was at her 100th birthday party in 1930. She died later that year. Her funeral was attended by more than 20,000 people.

Mother Jones was a true heroine of the working classes. She was born less than a half-century after the American Revolution and died on the verge of Franklin Roosevelt's New Deal. She lived through the presidencies of Andrew Jackson and Abraham Lincoln. She experienced the Civil War, the Spanish American War, and World War I.

Born in the era of the horse and wagon, she lived to see automobiles, trains, telephones, electric lights, radios, and motion picture films. She witnessed the United States make the dramatic change from an agrarian economy to an industrial economy. Standing about five feet tall and exuding a grandmotherly appearance, she appeared to be fragile and innocent. Her looks were deceiving however, for she was the passionate and energetic woman who indelibly impacted the American labor movement for years to come.

Today, her message lives on in the national magazine *Mother Jones*.

Sources

The information included in the chapter above was obtained, paraphrased, and/or quoted from:

http://www.spartacus.schoolnet.co.uk/USAjonesM.htm

http://digital.library.upenn.edu/women/jones/
MotherJones.html

http://www.kentlaw.edu/ilhs/majones.htm

MARGARET SANGER:
SHE INVENTED THE PHRASE
"BIRTH CONTROL"

MARGARET WAS ONE OF the bravest American women of the twentieth century. She embarked herself on a journey to fight for one of the most taboo issues of her time: birth control, a term which she, in fact, coined.

Margaret's passion for helping women started with the experience of growing up with a mother who got pregnant eighteen times and had eleven live births. Born in 1879 in Corning, New York, to an Irish born father and a Catholic Irish American mother, Margaret blamed the premature death of her mother at the age of fifty on the physical toll of having so many pregnancies. Margaret did not want to go through what her mother had gone through and in 1896 she attended Claverack College and Hudson River Institute. Afterwards, she joined the nursing program at White Plains Hospital in 1900.

By 1910, Margaret was married with three children and working as a public health nurse in the slums of New York City's Lower East side. There, she witnessed on a daily basis women dying at the prime of their youth from multiple childbirths and illegal abortions. These work experiences, combined with the premature death of her mother, made Margaret determined to do something about women's reproductive health.

At this time, Margaret and her husband were living within the pre World War I radical bohemian culture of Greenwich Village. They were part of a circle of intellectuals, activists, and artists that included Upton Sinclair, Emma Goldman, Max Eastman, John Reed, and Mabel Dodge. Margaret became a member of the Liberal Club, a supporter of the anarchist run Ferrer Center and Modern School, and an activist within the Women's Committee of the New York Socialist Party. From an ordinary nurse, Margaret had transformed herself into a revolutionary renegade.

In those years before World War I, lack of birth control left women (particularly poor women) deprived of their health, sexuality, and ability to care for children already born. Women grew old early in life because of the negative effects of multiple pregnancies on their bodies. They were giving birth to children that they could neither feed nor care for. Through laws pushed by religious leaders and accepted by physicians, sending contraceptive information through the mail was criminalized. This lack of birth control information disproportionately affected poor women in the slums who often did not even have an understanding of contraception. Unlike their poor counterparts, educated women had the means to get around the laws and were thus able to get contraceptive information as well as "French" products (condoms and other barrier methods) and "feminine hygiene" products (spermicides).

These hardships motivated Margaret to defy church and state and become the leader of the twentieth century campaign for reproductive rights. In 1912, she began writing a column on sex education, entitled "What Every Girl Should Know," which appeared in the New York *Call*. The columns included information about the functions of the body, sexuality, and reproduction. Her battle with the censors began soon afterwards when her column on venereal disease was labeled as obscene.

Margaret remained undaunted, however, and continued writing. Increasingly, she focused more on family limitation, a topic she was particularly drawn to after witnessing so many poor women suffer the pain of frequent childbirth, miscarriage, and abortion. Margaret was outraged that most women could neither obtain accurate information about contraceptives nor effective contraceptive devices. Without such information and products, women would never be able to secure freedom and independence. Influenced by the anarchist Emma Goldman, Margaret advocated for family limitation as a tool by which working-class women could liberate themselves from the economic hardships of unwanted pregnancies.

Soon, Margaret began to criticize the 1873 federal Comstock law and other similar state laws that prohibited the dissemination of information about contraceptives. In 1914, she began her own newspaper, *The Woman Rebel*, in which she defended women's reproductive rights, including the right to use contraceptives. Within months, three issues of *The Woman Rebel* were banned and Margaret was indicted for violating postal obscenity laws. To avoid criminal penalties, Margaret jumped bail and fled to Europe. En route to England, she got her friends to distribute 100,000 copies of a sixteen page pamphlet called *Family Limitation*, which provided detailed instructions on how to use various birth control methods. While in England, Margaret immersed herself within a circle of British radicals and feminists who helped her strengthen her social, political, and psychological justifications for family planning.

In 1915, Margaret returned to the U.S. to face the criminal charges that had been leveled against her the previous year. She thought that the media attention surrounding her public trial would create public support for family planning methods. Unexpectedly, however, Margaret's five-year-old daughter suddenly died, and a sympathetic public convinced the government to dismiss her case. Soon afterwards, Sanger began a nationwide tour to advocate contraceptives. She was arrested several times and attracted more and more public attention to birth control.

Until 1914, Margaret had been promoting contraceptives that women could obtain and use on their own, such as suppositories and douches. In 1915, however, a visit to a Dutch birth control clinic introduced her to the diaphragm, a form of birth control that was carefully fitted by medical personnel, the most effective contraceptive at the time. After her national tour in 1916, Margaret opened the very first birth control clinic in the country in Brownsville, Brooklyn. In order to inform the public about the clinic, Margaret and her colleagues handed out leaflets in different languages to women living in tenements. Women were coming to the clinic in droves and when the clinic was only nine days old it was raided. All the staff, including Margaret, were arrested. Margaret was imprisoned for thirty days. The publicity that the raid generated, however, brought Margaret a base of wealthy supporters that allowed her to build an organized movement for contraceptives. In 1917, she founded a new publication, *Birth Control Review*. In 1921 she began an educational and publicity campaign to build mainstream public support by starting the American Birth Control League (which in 1942 became the Planned Parenthood Federation of America).

Margaret had appealed her 1916 conviction, and although it was upheld, the New York court amended the laws and allowed physicians to disseminate contraceptive information if it was provided for medical reasons. This exception for medical reasons permitted Margaret in 1923 to open a legal birth control clinic, the Birth Control Clinic Research Bureau. This clinic became a model for all others to follow and served as a clearinghouse for data on the efficacies of various forms of contraception.

Despite this victory, however, Margaret knew that the fight was not over because women were still overly limited in their access to birth control. In 1929, Margaret formed the National Committee on Federal Legislation for Birth Control in order to reform the laws so that physicians could legally provide contraceptives.

Physicians, however, continued to be averse to contraceptives. Furthermore, Margaret encountered vehement opposition from the Catholic Church. Her legislative campaigns brought no immediate successes.

In 1936, however, the U.S. Court of Appeals did rule that physicians were exempt from the Comstock Law's ban on the importation of birth control, thereby allowing physicians to prescribe and provide contraceptives.

During the 1930s, Margaret became increasingly estranged from the birth control movement. In order to build more mainstream public support for the movement, the movement had toned down its radical feminism and focused more toward appealing to mainstream middle-class values. Margaret began to be viewed as too radical for the movement, and by 1942 she had resigned herself from active involvement with the movement.

At the end of World War II, however, Margaret emerged from retirement. After the war, there was increasing concern about international population growth, particularly in undeveloped countries. Margaret had traveled in the 1920s and 1930s to Europe and Asia to lecture on birth control. Now, in the post World War II era, she wanted to build an international birth control movement. Together with birth control advocates in Europe and Asia, she helped found in 1952 the International Planned Parenthood Federation.

Throughout her life as an advocate for birth control, Margaret was always on the lookout for ways to make birth control simpler, cheaper, and more effective. For example, she helped arrange the American manufacture of the Dutch-based spring-form diaphragms, which she had been smuggling from Europe. She also supported research on the development of spermicidal jellies, foam powders, and hormonal contraceptives. These efforts culminated in the 1950s when her help in securing crucial research funding led to the development of the first effective birth control pill.

Despite the advancements in the development of contraceptives, legal change was slow to follow. It was not until 1965, the year before Margaret's death, that the Supreme Court ruled unconstitutional the prohibition of contraceptive use by married couples. It was only in 1972 that the right to use contraceptives was also extended to unmarried couples. In 1973, abortions were made legal (and thereby safe), thus ending the horrific and illegal abortions of Margaret's time.

Some of Margaret's critics point out that she held some beliefs regarding eugenics that are outmoded by today's values. Many of these critics are members of the anti-family planning movement who have committed the fallacy of attacking the messenger (Margaret) rather than intellectually confronting those ideas of hers that have had a lasting and positive effect on our times. These critics often take Margaret's ideas, distort them, exaggerate them, and quote them out of context. Some critics have gone so far as to take pro eugenics statements and falsely attribute them to her. Most pro eugenics statements made by Margaret are, upon closer investigation, either statement not made by her or statements that have been grossly taken out of context and severely distorted. In the interest of honesty, however, it is fair to acknowledge and address those ideas of Margaret that are indeed outmoded by today's standards.

While Margaret unequivocally decried the racist exploitation of eugenics principles, she agreed with progressives of her era who favored: incentives for the voluntary hospitalization and/or sterilization of people with untreatable, disabling, hereditary conditions; the adoption and enforcement of stringent regulations to prevent the immigration of the diseased and "feebleminded" into the U.S.; and placing so-called illiterates, paupers, unemployables, criminals, prostitutes, and dope fiends on farms and open spaces as long as necessary for the strengthening and development of moral conduct.

These misjudgments of Margaret should remind us that no one is perfect and that all people are clouded by the limited vision of their time. The eugenics movement peaked in popularity during in the 1920s and 193s, and Margaret made the unfortunate mistake of adopting its language as a tactic. Nevertheless, discrediting the entire birth control movement because its founder did not perfectly embrace all of today's values is like discrediting the Declaration of Independence and U.S. Constitution because its creators, such as Thomas Jefferson, owned slaves and did not permit women to vote.

Today, the anti-family planning movement chooses to attack Margaret because it is easier to undermine the character of a long dead woman than confront the present-day message of the contemporary   problem of how many children to have and when to have them. As the futurist and historian H.G. Wells wrote in 1931, "The movement she started will grow to be, a hundred years from now, the most influential of all time. When the history of our civilization is written, it will be a biological history, and Margaret Sanger will be its heroine."

She died in 1966.

Sources

The information contained in this chapter was obtained, paraphrased, and/or quoted from:

http://www.time.com/time/time100/leaders/profile/sanger.html
(article written by Gloria Steinem)

http://www.nyu.edu/projects/sanger/msbio.htm

http://www.plannedparenthood.org/about/thisispp/sanger.html

RACHEL CARSON, THE GURU
OF THE ENVIRONMENT

RACHEL CARSON WAS BORN on May 27, 1907, in Springdale, Pennsylvania, a small community nestled around Allegheny River. Her sister Marian was eleven years old and her brother Robert was in the first grade when Rachel Carson came into the world. Her mother Maria was extremely proud of her little daughter and she started chronicling Rachel's childhood.

Early in her childhood, Rachel Carson wanted to be a writer. Her writing career began in 1918 when she published a story in *St. Nicholas Magazine*. The story came out of Carson's love of nature. Carson's interest in nature was inherited from her mother Maria who was instrumental in Rachel's intellectual and natural development.

Springdale was known for its quaint and rural charm but all of this was changed rapidly in the early nineteen hundreds. The Allegheny River allowed for iron to be sent to Pittsburgh. Many furnaces were located around the hills. Oil moved down the river as well and there was also wood from the heavy logging of the Appalachians. The river and the shoreline quickly became polluted.

By 1920, four of Carson's stories had been published in *St. Nicholas Magazine* and she was becoming increasingly sure that she would become a writer. Her literary success had a profound impact on her mother who was unhappy with her own life and wanted to make sure that her talented daughter should have the opportunity to fulfill her dreams. The family's economic and social status was hampered by Carson's father's inability to make enough money. Because of the Carsons' declining economic status, Carson adopted her mother's view that intellectual selfworth is more important than material wealth.

After graduating from high school, Rachel Carson enrolled at the Pennsylvania College for Women where her mother Maria continued to play a vital role in her daughter's life. This way Maria was able to participate in a college experience that had never been available to her. She even tried to avoid to being with her other two children who were having lots of personal problems—problems that proved too difficult for Maria to deal with.

Rachel Carson's sister Marian was married twice, the first time at the age of 17. She had two daughters, Virginia and Marjorie. They lived in the family house along with her brother Robert and his wife. Young Rachel Carson convinced herself that marriage is a hindrance in someone's life—the fact that was obvious to her by observing the life of her own family members.

In college, Carson focused all of her creative energies in the field of biology. Her interest in biology was intensified greatly by her adoring teacher Mary Scott Skinker, with whom she formed a lifelong friendship. Carson already had a broad understanding of wildflowers, birds and animals and her passion for preservation and conservation was already evolving.

After graduation from Pennsylvania College for Women, Carson applied to John Hopkins University for her graduation work in zoology. She applied herself intensely because she wanted to become a scientist and she used all her energy in that direction, just like she had four years earlier when she was trying to become a writer. Her imagination seemed most sparked by the ocean. She went to the Marine Biological Laboratory at Woods Hall in 1929, a research facility at John Hopkins, for a six week internship. The laboratory was the only educational center focusing on marine life at the time. The laboratory's library was well equipped with a variety of scientific journals from around the world as well as new books with all the most up to date information. Many of Carson's ideas developed from her time at the center.

In 1932, Carson graduated from John Hopkins, but even with her degree she could not find fulltime employment. She was able to teach summer classes at Hopkins where she started working on her doctorate. The Depression years were affecting the whole country, including the Baltimore-Maryland area, and finally Carson had to drop out as a doctoral candidate in order to devote her energy to a search for fulltime employment. Out of economic necessity, Rachel Carson returned to writing as the main source of her income.

In 1935, Carson started to work with the U.S. Bureau of Fisheries in Washington D.C. Her job entailed writing and producing a public educational series for radio. These programs were called "Romance Under the Waters." Carson began writing articles on marine life for many different publications after that.

Her research at the Bureau of Fisheries motivated her to embark on a new journey of writing and reporting on sea life.

By 1936, Carson had finished a brochure for the Bureau of Fisheries. Her supervisor was very impressed with her essay, "The World of Waters," and he appointed her as junior aquatic biologist with the bureau. Carson continued to work with the Fish and Wildlife Information Service all through 1946. But she was getting anxious to get back to her own writing. Her work with fish and wildlife was too consuming. She produced 12 booklets featuring the national wildlife refuge system which were called Conservation in Action.

To do the research for her government writing, Carson traveled across the country. Her travels convinced her that "preservation of wildlife and wildlife habitat" is a basic necessity for both man and animals.

Finally, in 1951, Carson's book, *The Sea Around Us*, on which she worked for many years, was published. It quickly hit the bestseller list. But there was resistance, both among readers and in the scientific community, to her message, because people were not ready to admit that a woman could deal with a scientific subject of such complexity. Nonetheless, Carson became a literary celebrity and even she was surprised with the success of the book.

In 1952, Rachel resigned her position from the Bureau of Fisheries to devote more time to her own writing. Rachel's mother Maria was always in her life until her death. When Rachel's sister Marian died, she became a guardian and fulltime caretaker of her sister's children, Marjii and Virginia. When Marjii became pregnant and gave birth to her son Roger in 1952, both the baby and the mother joined Rachel's household as well. Rachel's niece became ill in 1957 and when she died, Rachel became guardian of Roger because other family members refused to take any responsibility.

Her involvement with the Nature Conservancy and the American Foundation made Carson aware of how much her own personal efforts could help in saving and preserving the tracts of forest and shoreline.

Rachel was thinking about how to keep industrialists and developers from destroying the precious land around shorelines. This is how she developed the idea that has become quite commonplace now of raising money to buy private land so it would forever be preserved for public use.

Rachel Carson was not an opponent of technology. She was a scientist, after all. But she was concerned about the misuses of science. She became increasingly convinced that there were terrible effects from using synthetic chemical pesticides. Her years of working with and studying wildlife for the government made her very skeptical of synthetic pesticides. Even before 1945 she tried to interest *Readers Digest* in publishing an article on the use of the pesticide DDT. She was convinced that DDT and other synthetic pesticides had had a profoundly hazardous impact in the wilderness and in agriculture. But it would be a long time before any magazine tackled the controversial issue.

In 1957, a controversial program was started by the United States Department of Agriculture's fire ant eradication program. Many lawsuits were filed asking the department to halt the aerial spraying of private land with DDT. Many years later, of course, the use of DDT was outlawed.

By 1958, Rachel agreed to write a three-part essay for the *New Yorker* on the subject of chemical pesticides. As a result, she formed a network of scholars—scientists, journalists and activists who helped her to document a variety of environmental abuses. By gathering all the information on the subject, Rachel was convinced that an ecological crisis caused by misuse of pesticides endangered human health and wildlife.

But federal agents kept spraying the fire ants despite a growing protest by environmental groups and activists. Rachel was spurred on by all this in documenting the relationship between synthetic pesticides and human health.

Rachel had been working on a book for a long time that made her best case, but she was having trouble coming up with the best title. Finally in 1957 she named her book *Silent Spring* and it contained all her research on the harmful effects of pesticides. She had spent countless hours in the library of the National Institute of Health and as a result she was able to introduce hard evidence about the negative effects of pesticides on cells of the body and even the possible relationship with cancer. The more Rachel researched, the more she became convinced that understanding cellular metabolism was essential to understanding the chemical and physiological responses of the body to pesticides and to carcinogens.

She came to the conclusion that the relationship between pesticides and cancer was indisputable. She drew her conclusions not only from the voluminous files she had collected, but all the data in the scientific literature.

By 1960, Rachel was at the height of her analytical powers. She was completing chapters on the linkage of pesticides to wildlife from birds to insects to groundwater. She knew the public was ready to listen—and she was ready to take on all criticism.

But she was suffering great health problems by 1960, which only escalated in 1961, and it was only because of her indomitable spirit she was able to complete her masterpiece, *The Silent Spring.*

Rachel sent proofs of the copies of the book to many women's organizations and environmental groups. President Kennedy insisted she get invited to a conference on conservation at the White House. And finally, remember Readers Digest turning down the idea behind the book years earlier. Now *The Silent Spring* was being praised and excerpts being published in a number of magazines.

The Silent Spring caused outrage from the public who were enraged at the USDA's use of potentially dangerous pesticides. Further controversy was sparked by the chemical industry which derided her book as a gross "disappointment." They plotted their action against her. The National Agricultural Chemical Association issued its own pro pesticide propaganda booklet, "Fact and Fancy." By the summer of 1962, Rachel had finally reached the status of a distinguished public person. She was offered interviews with prestigious publications from many countries, and ultimately gave an exclusive interview to CBS Reports.

Rachel urged citizen activists to curb chemical industry abuses. She wanted new research into alternative methods of pest control. She called on grassroots activists to fight against the use of toxic chemical pesticides.

Needless to say the publication of *The Silent Spring* were not well received by the chemical industry, who spent hundreds of thousands of dollars to ridicule its finding.

But after CBS Reports aired, the New York *Times* came to Carson's defense and understood the important concept of defending the balance of nature against the assault being leveled at her.

CBS's producers had worked for months, interviewing not only Carson but interviewing other experts about pesticides and their potential dangers. The result was an erosion of support for government officials and a big low to the chemical industry.

The television network received a great outpouring of support for its report. Rachel herself received hundreds of letters. But most important of all, and most gratifying, was the support of Sen. Hubert Humphrey, D-Minnesota, who told her of his intent to conduct a congressional review of environmental hazards, including pesticides. Rachel was invited to testify before the newly formed Ribicoff Committee.

But her health continued deteriorating and by 1964 she was basically crippled by her disease. She died the same year—perhaps as a result of having grown up in such a badly polluted place.

IDA B. WELLS: JOURNALIST AND EARLY BLACK FEMINIST

LYNCHING OF THE BLACKS was one of the devices used to further secure the disenfranchisement of black men. Ida B. Wells, a black journalist from Tennessee, became the major force behind the international crusade against lynching. In her paper *The Memphis Free Speech*, she detailed the atrocities of lynching. The white male supremacists reinforced the dialectics of the lynch mentality by dehumanizing black males as rapists. This lynch mentality was embraced by white male and females because it was the right of the white man to protect white women from the rapists and therefore lynching was condoned.

Black women made some of their most important contribution to the cause of women's suffrage by crusading against lynching. Ida Wells, by exposing the horror of lynching, wanted to reach a larger international audience. Ida understood that she had to expose the lynching practices of the United States to the international community. She knew that the larger international audience had to be enraged in order to pressure the U.S. government to outlaw lynching. This opportunity came with the World's Fair in Chicago in 1893. Thousands of people from the United States and Europe attended the fair. However, the board of directors of the Exposition denied facilities for an exhibit to show the progress of colored people since Emancipation.

Ida B. Wells and Frederick Douglas raised the money to publish a booklet, "The Reason Why the Colored American is not in the World Columbian Exposition." Twenty thousand copies were distributed and the booklet was translated into French and German as well. This booklet explained the position of black people in the U.S. It also included an essay by Wells called "Lynch Law" in which she gave a detailed description of over a dozen atrocities. The authors argued that the reason for blacks being excluded from the exposition was to prevent the world from finding out that that black people are as intelligent and creative as white people.

Ida Wells went on two speaking tours in Scotland and England. During this speaking engagement she was able to raise a significant sum of money, which enabled her to wage her anti lynch campaign in the United States. While in Europe, Ida was able to establish an English anti lynching committee.

This crusade against lynching set the pace for the modern civil rights movement for blacks. By the end of World War I, the anti lynch movement had gained considerable momentum. Demonstrations were held all over the country, petitions were circulated, and lawsuits were filed. The movement helped to undermine the credibility of the racist appeal that black men were rapists and murderers.

THE SUFFRAGE MOVEMENT

THE ANTI-LYNCH MOVEMENT WAS waged together with the women's suffrage movement. The suffragist women in the National American Women's Suffrage Association (NAWSA) were committed to securing congressional approval of the 19th Amendment. The state-by-state ratification of the 19th Amendment began in 1913 during the Presidency of Woodrow Wilson.

During President Wilson's inauguration, thousands of women marched along Pennsylvania Avenue to demand the passage of women's right to vote. Although the women were attacked by a mob of white men, the marchers under leadership of Cary Chapman Catt kept marching on. Another group of more radical women led by Alice Paul engaged in a campaign of picketing and civil disobedience around the White House. A number of these women were arrested and placed in Washington, D.C. jails. During their incarceration many of these activists were treated harshly and even physically abused. While in jail, a number of ladies decided to embark on a hunger strike, an action noticed by the newspapers and other media outlets. It was apparent that all these extraordinary measures by the more militant women helped to hasten the urgency for ratification of the 19th Amendment.

Along with white women, black women participated as well in all of the activities aimed at securing women's right to vote. The first major action of black women was organized by Delta Sigma Theta, which is today a predominantly black public service sorority organization. However, the black women suffragettes in the 1913 protest marched under their own banner.

In March of 1914, the Susan B. Anthony Amendment (which would become the 19th Amendment) was set for hearing in the House and Senate committees where it had been previously stalled by southern legislators for twenty-five years. In spite of the effort of some of the sympathetic legislators, the amendment at this time failed to achieve the two-thirds and three-fourths majority required for passage of the amendment.

After a difficult campaign waged by NAWSA on the national level, the battle for women's right to vote was finally won in 1918 in the House and in the Senate on June 4, 1919. Once the victory for the right to vote was finalized, Carrie Chapman Catt summarized the meaning of the ultimate suffrage victory:

Following the ratification of the 19th Amendment, black women registered to vote in very large numbers. On the other hand, the opponents of the 19th Amendment did not lose any time in order to wage new attacks and restrictions over voting rights for women. Within a few days from the passage of the 19th Amendment, literacy tests, civil service-type examinations, birth certificates, and many other obstacles were invented to prevent black women from registering to vote. The legal recognition of suffrage rights was only the first step toward a long journey on the road to women's emancipation.

An essential point that has to be made when discussing the emancipation of women is that it was the longest in coming because the oppression of women has been the longest in its creation. The subjugation of women is the oldest form of human oppression whose origins can be traced back to several thousand years before Christ. By oppressing women, the class division in society was institutionalized where the women were literally reduced to the status of slaves.

By 1920, the number of women in the work force had doubled from four to eight million; still there were men who were demanding that these women return home to their families and children.

Emancipation of blacks was a monumental achievement. At the same time, this monumental event played an important role in delivering property rights for women. From this time on, workingwomen were paid their own wages and married men were not able to sell their property without consent of their spouses.

By 1870, the 13th, 14th, and 15th Amendments to the Constitution were ratified. The 15th Amendment had provided for black men's suffrage but not for women's right to vote. In 1872, Susan B. Anthony was arrested and convicted in New York City for trying to vote. When the Civil War ended in 1864, the anti-slavery movement was practically dissolved. Many veterans believed that their crusade had been completed. On the other hand, Anthony, Cady Stanton, and a score of other women, believed new initiatives and campaigns must be undertaken to secure the civil rights of former slaves and women. With the help of Anthony, the Equal Rights Association was founded in 1866.

This new organization was born out of a combination of common struggle that had been fought for thirty years to emancipate women. By removing the right to suffrage from the control of individual states, the 15th amendment provided the constitutional foundation for universal suffrage. This point did not escape the sharp eyes of Susan B. Anthony and others in the Equal Rights Association.

One of the first American suffragists, Anthony's contribution to the world was acknowledged in 1979 when she became the first women to have her image on a United States government issued coin. In 1866, she co-founded the National Women's Suffrage Association. She helped compile and edit the first four volumes of the history of women's suffrage from 1881–1902. She was the President of the National American Women's Suffrage Association (NAWSA). When she retired she turned her organization to her younger colleague Carrie Chapman Catt.

WOMEN'S RIGHTS
UNDER ATTACK

AT THE BEGINNING OF World War I in 1914 and throughout the 1920s, women were entering the workforce in large numbers, and these were not just single women. Many were married. By 1930 over 15 percent of all married women were working and the majority of these women were earning wages below the subsistence level.

However, during the Depression, working opportunities for all women, especially for middle class women, declined drastically. The general thought was that women had lost interest in work and professionalism, but this was not the reality. During the 1930s female membership in unions tripled from 265,000 to 800,000, including skilled and unskilled women workers. This right to unionize was secured for workers by the National Labor Relations Act in 1936. During the Depression years of the 1930s, young people were marrying at a much lower rate than usual and at the same time women were having fewer children and the fear of young women becoming pregnant was real. Women were consuming birth control products on a mass scale and contraceptives had become a big business in the United States in 1934. The demand for knowledge of birth control was growing among all women, whether middle class or working class. Women living in rural areas and the countryside were inquiring and asking for birth control as well.

In spite of some gains in the area of birth control, the battle for the right of reproductive choice was far from over. Margaret Sanger could not achieve the desired result from President Roosevelt's New Deal despite support from Eleanor Roosevelt. President Roosevelt was not ready to enrage the Catholic voters who totally were against any birth control initiatives.

By the late 1930s, it became evident that sexual attitudes in general had become on some level more liberal. Up to this point in time, most magazines viewed women's desire for birth control in a negative light. But in 1937, the *Ladies Home Journal* reported their research showed that seventy percent of American women were in favor of birth control and almost an equal number of women believed in the right to divorce.

As the United States was preparing to enter World War II, the demand for labor increased dramatically. The Roosevelt New Deal became popular and even patriotic. Women, students, and disabled people went into the labor force; still the need for labor was not met. The shortage of workers was ongoing and patriotic appeals were made to persuade stay-at-home mothers to take on full-time jobs. Mothers of young children were reluctant to join the labor force despite the fact that many mothers needed higher income. Young mothers did not seek employment in part because of the problem of childcare. A lack of childcare was responsible for too many latchkey children, and a high level of absenteeism. Pressure on the federal government to step in and pay for childcare centers bore fruit in 1943. That's when federal funds became available for childcare centers. However, the number of childcare spaces was limited, and the majority of women still had to make private arrangements.

The Second World War presented women in the United States with unprecedented opportunities to earn higher wages and learn and acquire new skills. Women became electricians, welders, ship fitters, pilots and other jobs that previously had been deemed fit for men only. At the same time, there was a tremendous shortage of men in institutions of higher education. The war effort created a vacuum in higher education, and opened ample opportunity for young women. The number of women getting degrees in law and medicine doubled and many young women were studying engineering. A significant number of women were moving from predominantly women's professions and entering banking, insurance, administration, and other business related occupations, which until then had been male dominated.

As workers in wartime industry, women found and developed new confidence in themselves. The growth of unionization continued to increase. A few trade union women were developing the concept of the Equal Rights Amendment for equal pay for comparable work. The United Automobile Workers (UAW) has a special division called the Women's Bureau, which was headed by Lillian Hatcher, a black autoworker. Lillian played an important role in the struggle for equal rights for women after World War II. Many women's groups and organizations such as the Capital General Federation of Women's Clubs, the National Association of Women Lawyers, and the National Federation of Business and Professional Women's Clubs embraced the demand for equality.

By 1945, with World War II over, most Americans thought it was proper for women to give up their employment and return to being full-time housewives again. However, most women workers wanted to continue their paid employment outside the homes. With a return of men from the battlefields, most companies required that all employees had to reapply for jobs. There were many more women than men applying for semi-skilled- and skilled jobs in manufacturing industries. However, most women were rehired in lower pay jobs, and this practice was implemented not only for working class women but also professional women.

Entering into the fray as well was the Red Menace, which was stirring and coming online full throttle. By 1946, the United States was in conflict with the Soviet Union. This was the year J. Edgar Hoover claimed that the Reds had infiltrated the American media and educational institutions. Joe McCarthy was elected Senator from Wisconsin and a group of extreme right-wing Republicans was gaining power and influence over the nation's political process and public policies.

By 1947, a conservative political and social climate was in place. Witch-hunts were everywhere. People who had been in any way progressive were under attack. Thousands of men and women of progressive tendencies were imprisoned in the anti-communist purges. Clerical workers and unions were especially picked out, because these workers were particularly active in seeking support for pay equity.

McCarthyism was an ideology that sought to destroy many of the progressive institutions that had come out of the New Deal, which were viewed by many Republicans as nothing less than communism. In their view, the New Deal was responsible for juvenile delinquency, divorce and broken homes. Sen. Joe McCarthy, R-Wisconsin, was a heavy drinker, gambler and womanizer, hardly a believable moral character. In spite of many of his shortcomings and his shady character, the McCarthy era promoted repressive legislation that promoted homophobia and gender oppression. How was it that such a thoroughly repulsive character as McCarthy was able to get such a popular response to his strange ideology? When the Soviet Union exploded its first atomic bomb in 1948, the entire leadership of the U.S. Communist Party was arrested and incarcerated. Among the arrested was Claudia Jones, a communist writer who was accused of trying to overthrow the American government by force.

The post-war U.S. after the long years of Depression was yearning for an ideal normal life. The media engaged in open hostility to feminists, portraying them as neurotics and subversives. There was a tremendous emphasis in the 1950s on the "essential differences" between men and women.

In 1949, *Fortune Magazine* released a poll that showed that close to 50 percent of Americans believed that college education for women should be merely preparation for marriage and family, and not a preparation for career and employment. On the other hand, during the same period, black women were entering colleges in greater numbers while many white women were marrying after completion of high school and dropping out of college.

Although the McCarthy witch hunt against communism was pretty much over by 1954, the extreme right never did abandon its anti-communist crusade. Phyllis Schlafly and her husband set up a foundation to inform

the world about the dangers of communism. McCarthyism was not only about politics, but it was also
about social conformity and the ideal of the family. All
through the 1950s, liberal academic women were again
accused of being left wing sympathizers and there was
an increase in attacks on homosexuals and lesbians.

At the same time, here were a number of visible
women in the political parties. Still, women lacked an organized collective voice on issues concerning women. In
1952 the women's division in the Democratic Party was
abolished and the Republicans made similar decisions.
Many women's organizations, which had their roots in
the better days of progressivism, were slowly disintegrat-
ing and their membership was dwindling. The Women's
Trade Union League was disbanded in 1950 as well.

From 1947 to 1954 the feminist movement was invisible. It appeared as if the lights had just gone out, and a
darkness was brought on by the conservative climate of
the time set in. Yet underneath, other things were stirring. A civil rights movement was brewing that would
rip conservative barriers down. It inspired the radical
social movements of the 1960s. In 1954, the National
Association for the Advancement of Colored People won
a major victory against the "Jim Crow" system of segregation. The Supreme Court ruled that segregated education violated the 14th amendment of the Constitution.
Pauli Murray, a lawyer and labor activist from the New
Deal, helped to win this judgment against segregation.
Pauli has demonstrated that the social, economic, and
psychological impact of a segregated system was not in
accord with the promise of equality.

While the feminist movement was at a standstill,
however, middle class women were gradually joining in

a wide range of community activities, which they saw as an extension of their domestic role. In the new suburbs, women helped to set up churches, schools, parks and libraries. The post World War II reputation for the dedication to family and children was over by the 1950s. It was obvious to many women that there was something wrong with the family structure, as the consumption of tranquilizers and alcoholism was rising and the divorce rate was skyrocketing. Family life became even more chaotic as teenagers started becoming rebellious nonconformists. Students all over the country were joining the organizations campaigning for civil rights. Teenage girls were looking for meaning in their lives. They felt that being an over protected white female had robbed them of significant and important life experiences.

ELEANOR ROOSEVELT, CHAMPION FOR HUMAN RIGHTS

ELEANOR ROOSEVELT BEGAN HER career as a political organizer in the 1920s with the Democratic Women's Committee. Her involvement there was a lifelong commitment. Promotion of full and fair employment and just wages was one of the mainstays of post war liberalism. President Truman appointed Eleanor to the United States delegation to the United Nations. She used her position to promote full and fair employment as part of what a democracy should have. She believed that on this issue the United States had to be of one mind. To Eleanor, it was extremely important that labor, management, and the government take actions compatible with this "world point of view."

She continued writing her column and publishing articles on the economy and other related issues. She was not afraid to expose those that she called "men and women of narrow vision" who were undermining reforms at home and were jeopardizing American prestige abroad. She criticized Congress, the President, and all politicians who followed the polls to determine their votes, rather than setting policy that is necessary for the people.

Eleanor endorsed full employment and price control legislation as solutions to major economic problems facing

107

post-war America. She believed that there were a number of approaches to the solution and not just one specific way to achieve democratic reforms. In her view, true reforms can be achieved only if the American public and political leaders tolerate dissent and promote free discussion of all ideas coming from different groups. She was asked to seek an election political office, but instead she chose to challenge party officials and members of Congress to embrace reforms because it was morally and politically necessary for the country.

With McCarthyism on the rise, Eleanor was afraid for the liberal wing of the Democratic Party and feared that the center of the party had confused liberalism with communism. Eleanor warned the president that Democrats cannot be more conservative than Republicans. The tension between President Truman and Eleanor was evident, but nevertheless she praised Truman's support for the Marshall Plan and lobbied diligently for its support within the United Nations. Although Eleanor disagreed with Truman on many issues, she gave him her endorsement in his re-election bid because she appreciated his boldness on some of the domestic issues such as fair employment and civil rights.

Eleanor defended civil liberties with the same enthusiasm that she tackled racial discrimination. She always believed in freedom of speech, the right to dissent, and the right to associate with whomever one wanted. From 1940 until her death in 1962, her position in civil liberties was clear. Whenever she could she always defended the liberties of Americans whose actions were questioned by the administration.

In spite of criticism from many sides, she never stopped expressing her views. On the other hand, President Roosevelt did not accept criticism easily when his policies came into question. The President ordered his staff to monitor the actions of fascists, fundamentalists, and other individuals who were attacking the New Deal. Eleanor's approach was different. She always said, "the real value of any democracy is the people's differences were valued and respected." A consistent theme in her speeches and writings was that the nation would reach its full potential only when it ceased to be afraid of dissent. She asserted: "When fear enters the hearts of people they are apt to be moved to hasty action" which will ultimately promote self-destructive policies.

Eleanor had a long history of commitment to anti-war activism. In the 1920s she campaigned for the United State's entry into the League of Nations and the World Court. She was a strong supporter of the Women's International League of Peace and Freedom and other women's reformist organizations. In her papers and articles she discussed economic reforms, which could serve as a deterrent to war. In 1938, Eleanor published *This Troubled World* in which she argued that the most efficient and profitable way to avert war is by negotiation and economic boycott, and not military conflict. In 1940, Congress passed the Alien Registration Act (known as Smith Act) whose primary function was to restrict Communist activism. Eleanor voiced her opposition against the House un-American Activities Committee. Eleanor became even more critical of HUAC in 1948 following the committee's announcement that communists had infiltrated American government and the industrial sector. She became outraged at the HUAC's practices of rounding people up without proper cause and called these blatant acts "Gestapo tactics."

Eleanor objected to the Committee's disregard of fundamental democratic principles and she was alarmed by the Committee's behavior which caused people to be scared of speaking up or even opening their front door because the state was monitoring everyone in order to arrest some it considered subversive.

After the Communist witch-hunt, HUAC launched attacks on the civil rights movement's leaders and associates. Eleanor once again expressed vocal counter attack on HUAC's activities. Unfortunately, most U.S. citizens were in agreement with HUAC and believed that the government had to take drastic measures against communists. With the escalation of Cold War rhetoric, the red scare became a large and sad part of post World War II America. The great majority of American people believed that communists should be stripped of their citizenship as well.

Ironically the majority of liberals sided with government on the issue of communists whose right to free speech and free association was outlawed. However, Eleanor continued to remind her listeners and readers to recognize the danger of their blind acceptance of anti-communist paranoia. She was aware that some people have a fear of what they don't understand. But she tried to explain that fear was a much bigger threat to society than dissent.

Eleanor used her column "My Day" to express her disbelief at politicians who overstepped the boundaries of their elected offices. In her opinion, Senator Joseph McCarthy, R-Wisconsin, was one of the biggest threats to American democratic principles. Although she despised Senator McCarthy, she felt even more strongly about president-to-be Richard Nixon. After he defeated

Helen Graham Douglas for U.S. Senate with the most despicable attacks, Eleanor was enraged by Nixon's claims that Helen Douglas was a Communist. Eleanor even encouraged Douglas to challenge the election by firing charges of voter fraud against the Nixon campaign. Eleanor recognized that Nixon's use of anti-communist hysteria and McCarthy's anti-communist witch-hunt propaganda had adversely affected the American people to the point that most Americans were willing to violate the first amendment's protection of free speech. When conservative Republicans started using the taint of communism to justify their opposition to the United Nations, Eleanor engaged herself in a one woman media blitz to rebuke the allegations. Just as McCarthy has used his skills in his anti-communism campaign, Eleanor used her own public relations and personal connections to bring information to the American public so that they could make informed and educated decisions. Eleanor believed wholeheartedly that the true test of democracy is the creation of a political climate in which differences are openly debated.

Eleanor stood up for her ideals all her life. All presidents, Democratic Party leaders, candidates for political offices, and civil rights and human rights organizations all sought her advice and they all fought for her endorsement. Eleanor knew that President Kennedy was the last Democratic president she would live to see in office. Although Kennedy was not her first choice, she was happy to see him elected because she saw in him great potential to implement many liberal ideas that she had worked on throughout her life. Eleanor was very pleased with Kennedy's inaugural address where he emphasized the need for service, human rights, and democratic values.

She was very excited about president's call for the Peace Corps, a concept she had been promoting since the 1950s. Eleanor died November 7, 1962, and she was buried in the rose garden of the Roosevelt estate in Hyde Park next to her husband, Franklin Delano Roosevelt.

THE SIXTIES: THE RISE
OF THE WOMEN'S LIBERATION
MOVEMENT

THE ADVANCES MADE DURING the early periods of the women's movement laid the basis for the explosion of feminism in the sixties. In spite of the distrust many felt toward feminism, most men and women shared its values by then. The very word feminism has been hard for many people to understand. Despite disagreement among women on the issue of feminism, however, almost all women believe that their daughters should have the same employment opportunities as their sons.

The sixties feminists shared the belief of their previous generations, and also a belief of a lot of sixties activists—and that was a spiritual and emotional commitment to the notion that the world could be a better place for all people; that such a thing was not only possible but inevitable. This new movement began with feminism's structural invention, which was a voluntary small group practice called "consciousness raising". Women spoke of their histories and their daily lives to each other in myriad consciousness raising sessions. And in the early sixties, the media consistently belittled it.

The feminist movement of the 1960s was known, of course, as the Women's Liberation Movement. This newly coined term continues to this day. From its early inception, the "movement" created outrage and reaction stoked by sensationalized media coverage. The reactionary forces never stopped belittling and demonizing not only feminism but all the political struggles of the 1960s.

The women who were instrumental in the development of the second phase of the Liberation Movement included Amy Kesselman, Heather Booth, Vivian Rothstein, and Naomi Weinstein, known as "the Gang of Four."

As women in the sixties recreated the feminism of an earlier period, many developed intense relationships. The Gang of Four began their work in Chicago and their contribution was instrumental in the emerging movement in the city. Building a successful women's liberation movement was a matter of survival for the politically and socially conscious women of the late 1960s. Women came together to articulate their anger and frustration about the political and social system in America. The main focus of the liberation movement was the fight for civil rights. The fight for civil rights was a universal one, including men and women, black and white. The liberation movement and the struggle for civil rights encouraged women to stand up for social justice. The civil rights movement has enabled many women to develop a vision of eradicating poverty and racism. And most importantly, these women wanted to change the existing power structure.

THE EFFECT OF THE ANTI-WAR & CIVIL RIGHTS MOVEMENTS ON MODERN FEMINISM

THE NEW LEFT ANTI-war movement was a terribly sexist place, and it helped form the feminism that evolved in the late '60s and '70s. The feminism of this time was also a direct response to the role of women in the middle class nuclear family of the 1950s. Since the first wave of the women's movement ended with the voting rights amendment of the twenties, very little had been done to advance the position of women in America. The disaffected teenagers and young women who were brought up in the 1950s became the major protagonists of the 1960s liberation movement. In the early 1960s the first major legislative advances for American women were witnessed. President John F. Kennedy, under the influence of Eleanor Roosevelt, established the first Commission on the Status of Women. In 1963 the U.S. Congress enacted the Equal Pay Act, authored by Edith Green, a House representative from Oregon. However, the most important step toward women's rights protection came from Title VII of the landmark 1964 Civil Rights Act. Title VII of the 1964 Civil Rights Act became the law that guaranteed for the first time equal employment opportunity for women. But this historic measure was the result of the efforts of many people over many years.

In June, 1965, following the confirmation of Title VII, President Lyndon B. Johnson appointed five people to the Equal Employment Opportunity Commission (EEOC,) the agency in charge of enforcing Title VII's provisions. Aileen Clarke Hernandez was the only woman appointed to the commission. Hernandez was a black woman and a divorcee. She was involved in the civil rights and trade union movements, and her previous job was as the Assistant Chief of the California Fair Employment Practices Commission. The new commissioners were given hundreds of pages of documents in order to orient them to the framework and duties of the EEOC. Hernandez noticed that there were only limited references to sex discrimination, all of which suggested minimal attention to the entire subject.

She observed that this insensitivity to sex discrimination was all too prevalent and she reported that a major meeting should be held to address these inadequacies. Even the liberals in Congress were not enthusiastic to add the sex provision to the Civil Rights Act because they feared it would prevent passage of civil rights for blacks. This Civil Rights Act was supposed to be "the Negro's hour" and therefore the women were excluded once again—just as had happened with the passage of the 14th amendment in 1886, which failed to provide women with the right to vote.

Michigan Congresswoman Martha Griffith challenged the inadequacies of the work of the EEOC and she was especially enraged about the practice in advertising columns that still labeled the jobs by sex.

The Citizen's Advisory Council on the Status of Women expressed its dissatisfaction with the EEOC's handling of sex discrimination complaints by women. Copies of Griffith's speech were distributed to the delegates of the state commissions during the Annual Conference of Commissions on the Status of Women in Washington, D.C. in 1966.

President Johnson carried the Civil Rights Act a step further by guaranteeing the civil rights freedoms to blacks. Title VII's guarantee of rights to women was an unintended by-product of the Civil Rights Act. Title VII of this bill barred discrimination in employment on the basis of race, color, religion or national origin, but did not mention sex. Howard W. Smith, a Democrat from Virginia and hard-line southern conservative had opposed the Civil Rights Act but nevertheless he submitted an amendment adding an additional basis: sex. Smith thought that by pairing the cause of black civil rights with the unpopular cause of women's rights he would prevent the passage of the entire Civil Rights Act.

Two women, Pauli Murray and Mary O. Eastwood, fought relentlessly to uphold the provisions of Title VII in the face of widespread resistance. This effort required endless hours of labor. Murray and Eastwood were active in early women's rights struggles at the turn of the 20th century. As a member of the President's Commission on the Status of Women, Murray was able to formulate a compromise in which the Commission could support the principle of gender equality. In addition to their commitment to ensuring the passage of Title VII in the Senate, Murray and Eastwood were among the twenty eight "founding mothers" of the National

Organization for Women. These two elderly suffragists
were the members of the old National Women's Party.

Title VII of the Civil Rights act provided for a federal
agency, the Equal Employment Opportunity Commission. The major function of this commission was to hear
complaints of bias in the workplace. In its first year, the
commission proved that sex bias relief in the employment place was desperately needed. A third of all complaints involved discrimination based on sex.

In spite of the many obstacles thrown up in the way
of Title VII, the fact remains a small group of women
had managed to change the fabric of the American
workplace within a decade. In 1972 the agency was
given the power to enforce its decisions in the courts,
and the coverage of Title VII was expanded to educational institutions that were previously excluded. In a
few years female airline "hostesses" won reversal of
policies that called for mandatory dismissal at marriage
or upon reaching the age of thirty five. Another victory
was made in the area of newspaper advertising where
there were separate heading for males and females in
Help Wanted listings. "Male" or "Female" categories in
the help wanted listings were abolished and craft unions
began accepting women who wanted to work as carpen-
ters, plumbers, and other professions that up until then
were male only.

As the war in Vietnam dragged on, women continued
to join the anti-war movement efforts as well as the civil
rights movement. University students were organizing under an umbrella called the Student Nonviolent
Coordinating Committee (SSNC). This committee has
inspired thousands of young people to join in the civil
rights movement. In 1964 hundreds of student volun-

teers joined the Mississippi freedom movement where they assisted blacks in voter registration. During the first years of the civil rights movement, women's rights had little meaning to many women. Within SSNC the treatment of women was unequal to that of men.

One of the women, Mary King, a white college student, made a decision to address the unequal treatment of women in her paper. The worldwide second class of women, which Simone de Beauvoir had brought to light in her book *The Second Sex*, made tremendous impact on women within the SSNC. The major theme of King's paper was to point out the assumptions of male superiority. In her paper, she pointed out that this male superiority was widespread and deep—in the same way white supremacy was. She pointed out that male superiority and white supremacy were equally detrimental to the equality of women. She pointed out that the women in the SNCC were competent, qualified and experienced and yet they were automatically assigned traditional "female tasks" such as typing deskwork, cooking, and other traditional women's chores. They were never given an equal position in day-to-day decision and policy making processes.

King and her former roommate Casey Hayden co-authored a second document on the topic of "unequal treatment of women in SNCC" and mailed the copies to many women who were active in the movement for social change. This memo came at a time when American women witnessed the upheaval of the largest and most powerful feminist movement in the U.S. The two women who authored the memo had no idea that their statements would have such a profound effect on the women who read them.

Building a significant and powerful women's rights movement was a very complicated and complex task because so much has to be learned and changed in personal relations between men and women. Within the movement itself there were questions about the relationships of men and women that needed to be resolved—who should do secretarial work, leadership work—who should act as a spokesperson. There were problems not only between men and women, but there were also problems between white and black women whose life experiences and circumstances were dissimilar. These issues had a negative impact on the movement itself, and were not easily resolved.

The civil rights movement and the anti-war movement against Vietnam were evolving simultaneously. From 1968 to 1970, Naomi Weinstein and her colleagues played an active role in organizing women in a variety of groups and identifying issues of common interest. Naomi also helped organize a number of activities against the war. Women were questioning whether marriage and having babies were the only things that the women wanted to do with their excellent education.

The liberation movement energized women to organize and to confront head-on all forms of sexism in their lives. Most importantly, they were challenging the power relations between genders in private lives as well as in social institutions. The idea that "personal life" is political and therefore what is private has its political origin was novel. Especially because political change only happens through collective activism. Women in the liberation movement had strong connections and emotional ties with all people who are struggling against injustice. If women were to achieve their full liberation they would have to defend the legitimacy of the independent women's movement that was constantly under attack on all fronts.

Naomi and several of her friends wrote a women's history play which they named "Every Woman" and with this play they hoped to bring all people together to join the great cause that women have embarked on.

I'm all women, I am every woman. Wherever women are suffering, I am there. Wherever women are struggling, I am there. Wherever women are fighting for their liberation, I am there.

I am at the bedside of the women giving birth, screaming in labor; I am with the woman selling her body in Vietnam so that her children may eat. I am with the woman selling her body in the streets in American cities to feed the habit she acquired from her boyfriend.

I am with the woman bleeding to death on the kitchen table of a quack abortionist. I am with all women; I am all women and our struggle grows.

And where there are women too beaten down to fight, I will be there; and we will take strength together. Everywhere, for we will have a new world, a just world, a world without oppression and degradation.

The play promoted a shared feeling of vision, unity, and hope among women. Women's liberation union was emphasizing action and involvement of people of all political persuasions.

Barbara Emerson was a young black woman activist who started her journey to womanhood in 1963 in Georgia. Her father, Hosea Williams, was a civil rights activist. Still, Barbara learned about the civil rights movement like most of the rest of us, through television, with its powerful images of lunch counter sit-ins, dogs attacking demonstrators, and children and young adults being knocked down against buildings by the policemen because they were protesting segregation.

But she also learned about them in a more in-your-face kind of way. Of course, for blacks the Civil Rights Movement was about more than images; it was the movement against segregation, which was real and personal. Barbara remembered vividly the Jim Crow laws where cars on the trains were specifically marked "Colored Only." Barbara remembered crowded waiting rooms at the train station and a need for the blacks to bring their own lunch because they were not allowed in the dining car.

The number of individuals joining the movement was growing daily as more and more people of all ages—adults, senior citizens, and especially young people—got the strength and inspiration to join the movement. Teenagers and young people received their motivations from songs like "Oh Freedom" and "Ain't Gonna Let Nobody Turn Me Round." The participants of the civil rights movement were inspired by non-violent tactics, and many were willing to be arrested. Young people did not mind being arrested in order to end the segregated parks, movies, restaurants, schools, libraries, and all other public and private facilities. In 1963, during the historic march on Washington, over 200,000 Americans of all races demanded legislation to end discrimination in education, housing, and employment.

Not long after the march on Washington, in 1964, Congress passed a major civil rights act to prohibit discrimination in public places and employment. Slowly the civil Rights Movement was beginning to gain some positive results.

March 7, 1965, when demonstrators in Selma were attacked by state troopers, was known as "Bloody Sunday." When the news showed the brutality used against the demonstrators, many people were appalled. The Bloody Sunday event did not discourage Barbara, her father, and thousands of others who cared about freedom for blacks, from taking part in the march to Montgomery on March 21, 1965.

They engaged in a 50 mile long march to Montgomery to protest the denial of voting rights for blacks who had attempted to register to vote in Selma. In 1965 the Senate passed the capital Voting Rights Act, providing for federal examiners to oversee voter registration and elections.

The women in the liberation movement, of course, saw that securing full human rights for women would require extraordinary means and commitment to bring it to completion as well. This respect for women pertained to every aspect of society and it seemed that many women took their perceived inferiority for granted. For this reason many women saw the need to identify themselves as women and to connect with other women if they were to overcome the stereotyping and the treatment that resulted from that.

Over the centuries, women have been convinced that it is their role to serve others. Self-sacrifice is their highest aspiration, it would seem. Many women remain psychologically vulnerable to the accusation of being "selfish" if they requested something for themselves. Women understood early enough that if they were to gain respect and equality with men the basic behavior and psychology toward women has to be changed as well. Women in the liberation movement knew that changing the behavior and psychology of many men would be difficult if not impossible and they were aware that direct confrontation with men was eminent. Women had to prepare to fight for liberation by defeating the whole system of female subservience. Women were determined to level the playing field of men in relation to women.

The major goal of the liberation movement was to reach full human rights, which would enable women to decide for themselves what a woman wants out of life and then to work hard to bring this idea to reality. Women were not seeking to live like men; they were seeking something much higher—their own authenticity. The women who participated in the liberation movement in the 1960s were no longer able to ignore the contradictions when men insisted that women must occupy an inferior social status.

The groundwork for this new revolutionary movement that women were embarking on was laid out by Betty Friedan. Men were invited to join the movement only if they genuinely cared about social justice, but the visionaries and leaders of this social revolution were to be women. Society as it was structured had too many privileges for men and it was not likely that they would be willing to change it in any meaningful way. The women saw that it was up to them to remake society on the model of the true interdependent community.

The media image of feminists was distorted, depicting them as unattractive and bitter women who could not get men. This media distortion of feminist women frightened off women for decades and continue to do so to this day. Many women were prepared to call themselves feminists, but chose to disassociate themselves from the movement because many were afraid to take the risks of alienating men. Another controversial issue that the media took out of context was the feminist idea of celibacy. Some feminist believed that celibacy was an appropriate alternative to abusive relationships. Although the women in the movement did not condemn good sexual relationships or worthwhile family life, at this historical moment many women felt that the sacrifices had to be made if women are to achieve a true revolution. As in any revolution there is a tremendous need of time and energy and women had to be free of all other obligations in order to secure the better way of life for all women. The feminists of the 1960s and early 1970s thought that in a few years they would be able to bring the world down through their revolution. They never imagined the struggle for women's rights and equality would go on for twenty years, forty years, or even longer. For these reasons the "personal life" was downplayed, believing that there would be plenty of time to live a normal life after the revolution was won.

One of the most important contributions that the liberation movement made was promoting martial arts training, thus enabling women to defend themselves physically from the random violence committed against them everywhere, including homes and public places. But like everything else, this position for self-defense was under attack, accusing the women in the movement of promoting violent behavior among women. This was an absurd statement made by the anti-feminists forces. Clearly, the purpose of martial arts training was to stop the intended violence against women by making it more dangerous for the would-be assailant.

By 1969 there were numerous women's organizations all over the country. Some were independent from each other, but informally they were all related by their intentions. Ideas traveled fast in the women's movement the same way they were in the anti-war movement. People were traveling a lot and disseminating ideas. The more radical wing of the movement was leaning more toward separatism from men. The idea for separatism was understandable at the time, given the extent of male domination of the anti-war movement. Many women were ambivalent about feminism because not all women in general shared the same life experiences. The women's movement consisted overwhelmingly of young, white, middle to upper middle class, mostly university educated women. Other groups emerged on the scene simultaneously such as Black Power, the beginnings of La Raza and that of the American Indian movement. The women in the movement were concerned about war, poverty, and race issues, and those ideas of the movement were the place where feminist felt relieved to discuss these problems.

THE NATIONAL ORGANIZATION FOR WOMEN—CHAMPION OF EQUAL RIGHTS FOR ALL

THE PRESIDENT'S COMMISSION ON the Status of Women was dissolved in 1963 and state commissions on the status of women were set up all around the country. In 1966 Betty Friedan came to Washington, D.C. for the National Conference of Representatives of State Commissions.

Long before the conference, women's rights advocates had worried that the survival of the sex provision of Title VII was at risk. Betty Friedan pointed to the efforts of many who were trying to undermine the effectiveness of the EEOC. A number of the state commission members urged the formation of a feminist pressure group. Following a heated debate, Friedan introduced a measure for setting up an independent women's advocacy organization. However, the majority of the women that attended the meeting rejected the idea of an independent women's organization in favor of working within existing governmental processes. A few of the delegates who had attended the Friedan meeting tried to introduce a resolution to the EEOC to enforce its provisions related to sex discrimination in employment. The women were

informed that they did not have the power to take any
action in ending employment discrimination based on
sex. When the women in the group heard that they had
no power to even pass a resolution, they came to an immediate conclusion that a new organization for women
was essential.

Leading the conference was a small number of women
who held prominent positions in government mostly from
the Women's Bureau and the Department of Labor. These
women followed closely the work of EEOC, convinced
that this governmental body had failed to enforce the
prohibition against sex discrimination in employment.
These women had come to the conclusion that there was
a need for an organization that would be a voice for all
women just like civil rights groups had done for blacks.

Twenty eight women who met on the final day of the
Third National Conference of the Commission on the
Status of Women planted the first seed for an organiza-
tion for women.

The laws that existed did not give priority to sex discrimination cases. The limits were passed and the EEOC
was to dispose of the cases of sex discrimination within
sixty days. Hernandez had been applying pressure to
the Commission to act on the cases for months and she
went even to the White House to present her concerns.
The administration was slow in responding to any of
Hernandez's concerns; the administration even was de-
laying the replacement of the new commissioners.

At the closing luncheon of the status of women conference, a small rebellious group founded the National
Organization of Women. The members of this newly
created organization saw the need for more radical
solutions to end discrimination against women. They

saw that any proposals made by the President's Commission on the Status of Women were inadequate. On October 26, 1966, during the first organizing conference of NOW, Betty Friedan was elected its first president. In one year, NOW membership grew from 300 to 1,200. During the national convention of NOW in 1967, the organization endorsed reproductive rights, which spelled out the specific rights of women to choose and to control her own child-bearing, including access to birth control and abortion.

The statement of the organization proclaimed that:

We, men and women who hereby constitute ourselves as the National Organization for Women, believe that the time has come for a new movement toward true equality for all women in America, and toward a fully equal partnership of the sexes, as a part of the worldwide revolution of human rights, now taking place within and beyond our national borders.

The purpose of NOW was to bring women into full participation of the mainstream of American society. In the view of NOW leadership, the time had come to confront, with concrete action the conditions preventing women from enjoying the equality of opportunity and freedom of choice that were their rights as individual Americans, and as human beings.

The 1950s and 1960s brought profound changes in America society, and those changes made it possible to advance further the unfinished inclusion of women toward true equality.

By this time the lifespan of women had extended to seventy-five years and it was no longer necessary or possible for women to devote all their lives to child rearing. In spite of this fact childbearing and raising children was still used to justify preventing women from equal professional and economic participation.

Despite all the talk about the improved status of American women, the actual position of women was declining through the 1950s and 1960s. By the late 1960s nearly fifty percent of all American women were working outside the home; however, the overwhelming majority worked in traditional women's industries. As a consequence, full time women earned an average of sixty percent of what men earned, and the wage gap had been increasing during this period. About two thirds of black women workers were in the lowest paid service occupations.

Although discrimination in employment on the basis of sex was prohibited by federal law through Title VII of the Civil Rights Act of 1964, the EEOC made no clear intention of enforcing the law on behalf of women. Many cases of discrimination were black women who had been the victims of the double discrimination. Here it is very worthwhile to reiterate the ending statement of the purpose of NOW:

We believe that women will do most to create a new image of women by acting now, and by speaking out on behalf of their own equality, freedom and human dignity not in enmity toward men, who are also victims of the current half equality between the sexes but in an active, self-respecting partnership with men. By so doing, women will develop confidence in their own ability to determine actively, in partnership with men, the conditions of their lives, their choices, their future, and their society.

The creation of NOW played a big role in the formation of another important new left organization—Students for a Democratic Society. The goal of SDS included the eradication of racism and poverty, more student control in college and universities, and withdrawal of United States forces from Vietnam. Yet women in the student movement, just like women in the liberation movement, were ridiculed and verbally abused and the slurred phrases were constantly used, such as: "She just needs a good screw."

By 1966 the number of women's caucuses and workshops intensified and in June of 1967 a statement was drafted in the women's liberation workshop that challenged the males within the SDS by calling upon them to root out "male chauvinism" within the organization.

The 1967 Convention results were printed in New Left Notes. This was one of the earliest documents that used the term women's liberation. A committee was set up in the National Council to develop an analysis of the exploitation of women as producers and consumers and to present and report to the National Council where concrete proposal and changes were to be made.

This document read:

We seek the liberation of all human beings. The struggle for liberation for women must be a part of the larger fight for human freedom. We recognize the difficulty our brothers will have in dealing within male chauvinism and we will assume our full responsibility in helping to resolve contradiction. Freedom now! We love you!

By 1968 women in every city around the country were getting together in groups to discuss gender bias and discrimination, and finding ways to overcome it all. The phrase "women's liberation" was widely accepted because so many women stayed away from calling themselves feminist because the word feminist portrayed women in a very negative way.

Some groups had a firm belief that no matter how progressive men seemed to be, they would not give up their privileged status voluntarily. For these groups in the movement, men could not be counted on as true allies in the fight against sexism and gender discrimination. If women wanted true freedom and equality, they realized that women would have to organize a fight for their rights by themselves. These women saw that the only way to get their full freedom was by restructuring of the whole of society. As the women were in an unequal relationship with men, the restructuring of society was only possible by changing the relationships between genders.

Women in the liberation movement realized that it was important for women to share their experiences with each other. By discussing these common experiences, the women could identify many psychological modes of domination in and out of homes. And in order to reach the full spectrum of women, these findings, opinions, and work of women in the liberation movement had to be published.

Just like slavery, women's oppression was an integral part of the social and political system and that system had to be broken down.

Women had to learn about their own history, which was the only way to break down the myth that women were inferior human beings to men. For centuries the rulers, for whatever reasons, consciously or intuitively, omitted female or black history from the textbooks. Many courageous women in the movement brought this inequality of history out, paving the road for freeing women from centuries long bondage.

None of it would have been possible without the early suffragettes. Because of them, women were uniting again to achieve their final liberation and human rights. Male supremacy is the oldest form of domination and oppression. All power structures throughout most of the history have been male dominated and they kept this control by use of military and physical force.

To unite women to stand up against male oppression the major task was development of a female "class consciousness" by exposing the sexist foundation of all institutions. The women in the movement were committed to doing whatever was necessary to ensure that every woman had an equal chance to participate politically and an opportunity to develop her full potential.

A great deal of confusion existed all through the 1960s and 1970s about the role of the women's liberation movement. During the 1960s, hundreds of women's groups began emerging, but there was a wide variety of them, with a number of conflicting ideologies. The number of women's groups alone suggested how desperate women were to escape their own oppression.

Critics of the movement asserted that most women in the movement were "middle class" white women, a fact no one can deny. Most of the radical women in the movement were young, college educated, and very sophisticated in their thinking. These young women were not married yet; they had no children: and they didn't believe that it was necessary for them to be married in order to support themselves.

The meaning of the liberation movement did not mean the same thing to all women because the conditions, life experiences, and social and economic circumstances were different among the various ethnic groups. Many radical women accepted the attitude of men in the movement who sneered that that women's liberation was mostly middle class and subjective. The forms of oppression experienced by middle class women and students were different from class oppression in general. In other words, the non-radical women believed also that women should organize around women's oppression, but only as an integral part of a more inclusive approach to the struggle against racism and economic exploitation of the working class.

The women's liberation movement had progressed to the point that it demands an end to the living conditions and misery most women suffer daily. These include, but are certainly not limited to:

—lack of birth control information in high schools

—poor provisions for maternity leave and childcare facilities for working women

—unequal pay and unequal rank in unions and work places

—no bargaining rights or security for waitresses, office workers, store clerks, hospital and nursing home workers, and other professions in which women attempted to participate.

The majority of women in the liberation movement started their activism in the male dominated left and because many of these women could not tolerate the "blatant sexism" of the New Left, they reacted by embracing the predominantly feminist organization. One of these was Robin Morgan. Morgan was an activist in the liberation movement as well as a writer and editor for new left alternative cultural newspapers in New York City. One of these papers was called *Rat* and because of the paper's bias, Morgan refused to write for this male dominated and sex biased paper. In 1970, Morgan, with other women, took over *Rat*. Morgan was a very proficient writer and in a 1970 anthology of feminist writings, *Sisterhood is Powerful*, she was able in her articles to define the meaning and goals of the early movement for hundreds and thousands of people. Morgan's international feminist anthology *Sisterhood is Global* was printed in 1984. In 1990, Morgan became editor-in-chief of *Ms.* Through her writings she was able to demonstrate her passionate concerns for the lives of women everywhere.

Morgan and many other feminist writers of the time exposed in their stories the practices and beliefs of the male dominated Left. The majority of males in the left were claiming that they knew what women liberation was, yet continued to degrade women by almost everything they said and did. The male writers of the Left were calling the women in the liberation movement many demeaning names. They used such expression as "pussy power," "hairy cunt," "groovy cunt," and "crazy cunts." For the most radical feminists, the language showed the serious limits of their understanding. By analyzing the behavior and actions of the male dominated movement, it became obvious that a legitimate liberation of women could only be led by those who had suffered the oppression. This is true of black women, brown women and white women. Men would have to learn to relate to these issues. Women realized that no one's suffering is ever irrelevant.

Uniting women from different racial and social backgrounds was a difficult task. Even though black women and white middle class feminists agreed on the principle of gender equality, the two groups of women were divided on a number of issues. The white feminists saw paid employment as a way for women's independence and self realization, but black women who had to work regarded jobs as a task, something they were forced to do in order to survive and to feed their families. The condemnation of men by some of the white radical women did not play well with black women because of their bond with black men who were partners in the struggle against racism. White feminists were against all restrictions over abortion, while black women feared that abortion and sterilization would be over-used in the black community. Most importantly, the social issues that were vital to black women were not dealt adequately by existing feminist organizations.

Black women's activism was nothing new. There were many well known black women who had been involved in the American Civil War of the 1860s such as Sojourner Truth, Harriet Tubman, Frances E. W. Harper, Edith B. Wells, and Mary Church Terrel. The black feminists of the civil rights movement were a continuation of countless generations of sacrifice and hard work.

There were only a small number of black women in the women's liberation movement in the 1960s. By early 1970s an effort was made within the black community to draw black women together. As a result many clubs and organizations were formed on campuses, and clubs and workshops were organized wherever possible. In 1973, in a meeting of black women in New York City, the National Black Feminist Organization (NFBO) was founded. During its best time the organization had about 2,000 members but by the end of 1970 it was dissolved. The hundreds of women who joined the ranks of NFBO were previous activists from the new Left, civil rights, and early women's liberation movement.

The women in the black feminist movement had many more obstacles to overcome than the white women because they had to struggle against racism and sexism at the same time. And the male dominated media in the 1960s and 1970s had been especially detrimental to the cause of women's liberation for third world women, especially black women. As the liberation movement was characterized exclusively as the white middle class movement, black women who joined had been seen rather as a "dividing the race."

Black women had suffered profound cruelty from the time of slavery in the United States and this had not stopped in the 1970s. Being black and female in America meant suffering double discrimination in a country that was racist and sexist. Black women had been called "matriarchs" by white racists and black nationalists because the black women were strong and very vocal in their thinking. In order to survive the horrendous living situation during slavery, women had to be strong—because their survival depended on their personal strength. After the abolition of slavery, black women were the main breadwinners in the family.

The reaction of black men toward the feminist movement was very negative as well. For blacks, the organizing of black women might have meant that black men would lose valuable white male allies in their struggle. At the same time, black men realized that they had to change their habitual sexist ways of oppressing black women. So these divisive behaviors of black males had a powerful effect in deterring the growth of an independent black women's movement.

For the first time in modern history the problem of the subordination of women and the need for their liberation was seriously recognized by some socialist thinkers in the twentieth century. In the nineteenth centuries there were a number of studies that stressed the importance of the issue of women's subordination, but at this time there was not any real theory that provided a viable solution to the problem. Therefore it was up to women to develop their strategies for overcoming the discrepancy and the treatment of women in society. For most women in the liberation movement, de Beauvoir's work, *The Second Sex*, was the greatest single contribution on the subject of women's inequality.

Schulamith Firestone's piece, "The Dialectical Sex," was an early and thoughtful piece of work which helped the women in the liberation movement develop and shape their radical ideas. The biological division of the sexes for reproductive purposes was where much of it began. The biological and psychological divisions were what allowed men and women to develop only half of themselves at the expense of the other half.

The major goal of feminism was to create an alternative system that would free women from the tyranny of their reproductive biology. Family planning was imperative for the women. Before the new methods of contraception, multiple childbirths caused severe female reproductive problems and premature deaths. The feminists were not against marriage but they were against marriage and family that promoted the sexual repression of women.

THE POLITICS OF THE 1970S & THE MYTH OF THE HAPPY HOUSEWIFE

B Y THE 1970S, THE myth of the so-called happy American housewife was broken. In her book, *The Feminine Mystique*, Betty Friedman exposed the prejudices against working mothers by pointing out that stay-at-home women were turning to alcohol, tranquilizers, and other vices for comfort. By this time it seemed that the direction of equality of women was favorable for many women. In 1973 the Supreme Court ruled that Jane Roe's denial of a safe abortion was unconstitutional. Support for women's rights extended in the political arena as well. Bella Abzug, Betty Friedman, and Representative Shirley Chisholm, formed the National Women's Political Caucus and as a result 1972 was proclaimed "Year of the Woman."

Also in that year, a record number of women were elected to higher political offices. The decade would be marked with an extraordinary amount of political creativity. The struggle for abortion rights had paid off, and the lives of women were further politicized by bringing to the public agenda the issue of sexual harassment, rape, and domestic violence. A new generation of radical women were requesting Women's Studies departments at many universities.

The advocates of women's rights and women's liberation still had to face formidable opposition along the way. The media has greeted the new feminists and liberation movement with ridicule. The feminists of the 1970s were not overly concerned by the negative portrayal of their activism by the mainstream media. The feminists countered the mainstream media's influence with the alternative papers and at the same time applied pressure to all major media outlets to print articles by women writers. When Gloria Steinem started *Ms.* magazine, she proved that there was a significant market for women's journals. By 1973, *Ms.* had a subscription list of 200,000 people.

In addition to fighting the power of the media, women in the liberation movement had to face other forces attacking their credibility such as the Catholic Church and extreme Protestant and Jewish groups who also were challenging abortion rights.

By the early seventies, anti communism had lost its demonizing power. The civil rights movement had become a powerful engine, fueling groups, both white and non-white. There was a great emerging of groups onto the political scene, protesting the historic injustice of white colonization. Times were also getting tougher for poor woman, and black, Asian American, and Chicana feminists were organizing. As a result of these so-called cultural feminist issues, the farm workers' movement, welfare rights, undocumented workers and prison rights groups were emerging. The cultural feminists brought to light the issues of the poor migrant women and families, far removed from the white feminist movement.

The Equal Rights Amendment was defeated because the 1960s liberation movement faced the bizarre complaint that its passage would lead to moral decline in general. Anti-ERA women grew fearful as they watched anti-war activists, students, professors, civil rights marchers, and young women rebelling against the norms of personal behavior by flaunting long hair, using coarse language, and displaying tacky clothing.

On a more personal level, the female opponents of the ERA feared that if feminist values became constitutional it would mean the end of their Bible-based way of life. Most of these women were active members of fundamentalist and evangelical churches. Their understanding of the Bible was that women were to be responsible for home and family and their position was always submissive to that of their husbands.

Congress had voted to submit ERA to the states on March 22, 1972. Hawaii was the first state to ratify it. Within seven days, six more states ratified the proposed amendment and the supporters of ERA were confident that the required thirty eight states would follow suit by the end of the year.

THE RELIGIOUS RIGHT
AGAINST ERA

HOWEVER, THERE WAS OPPOSITION to ERA from an unexpected source. The Phyllis Schlafly Report for February 1972, " What's Wrong with the Equal Rights Amendment?" had already been mailed to a number of women in Oklahoma. This report inspired Ann Patterson, who became the leader of the anti-ERA movement in the state.

On March 29, 1972, the ERA failed by a vote of 52 to 36 in the Oklahoma House of Representatives. This was the first major setback in the ERA ratification. The women opposing ERA were not prepared for the fight, but Schlafly was. The anti-ERA movement was born after the defeat in the Oklahoma legislature. With the anti-ERA movement the nucleus of the pro family movement was born. With help Phyllis Schlafly in St. Louis, Ann Patterson from Oklahoma contacted conservative women in other states. Patterson was very pleased with the results. Most of the states that she called "stopped or slowed down the ratification process, although some ratified it later."

Despite the first defeat of ERA, the proponents of a national movement had no reason to doubt that it would not be quickly ratified. Twenty two states ratified ERA in

1972 and by the end of 1973 there were thirty states in favor of the amendment. But after 1973, the pace almost stopped. From 1974 until 1982, only five more ratifications were obtained, bringing the total to thirty eight. At the same time, five of the ratified states had voted to rescind their previous decision. After ten years of struggle, ERA was still three states short of the necessary three quarters of the states, or thirty eight states, that were required for ratification.

The ranks of the anti-ERA movement in Oklahoma were swelled by members of Churches of Christ. The anti-ERA campaign brought together people whose religious backgrounds were different and who would otherwise not have met. Patterson's arguments against ERA were mostly legal, not religious. Most of the anti-ERA activists emphasized the religious reasons for opposing ERA, but Patterson was organizing women under a slogan as "Women for Responsible Legislation." The first vote went their way, but they knew the future outcome would depend on how they presented their case in the hearings.

Ann Patterson and Beverly Findley headed up an organization from the Church of Christ. It began recruiting members and activists for their campaign. Anti-ERA activists in Oklahoma were also recruited from the John Birch Society, the Republican Party, and most importantly, the Oklahomans from Phyllis Schlafly's mailing list. The John Birch society magazine *American Opinion* opposed ERA, and also opposed gay rights, childcare programs, public education, and feminism. Based on their ideology, its members were targeted as source of recruits to oppose the ERA and other related liberal or feminist causes.

The Baptist Church, the Church of Christ, the Mormons, also shared a staunchly conservative family policy, and these churches were also fertile grounds for anti-feminist activists. The appeal against ERA was based in great part on Phyllis Schlafly's insistence that the ERA had to be opposed to save the traditional family.

At the beginning, Stop ERA was not a national organization. It was a collection of many local and state groups. All this changed in 1975 when Schlafly invited her subscribers to join a new organization, Eagle Forum, which labeled itself as the alternative to "women's lib."

In 1977, Schlafly began a project for the Eagle Forum in which she said librarians and feminists were denying equal rights to pro-family books. With this gimmick, Schlafly was able to bring together under one umbrella all of the scattered ad hoc organizations into one national organization. She made sure that all members were provided with information needed to persevere in their quest to defeat ERA.

THE STORY OF BETTY FRIEDAN AND *THE FEMININE MYSTIQUE*

B ETTY FRIEDAN WAS BORN in Peoria, Illinois, on February 4, 1921, just one year after women were given the right to vote. She was born Betty Naomi Goldstein, and was the daughter of a Russian Jewish immigrant jeweler and a former newspaperwoman. Betty's parents raised her to be a very self-confident, bright young woman with dreams of attending college and one day having a family.

Betty's mother encouraged her daughter to pursue journalism. Betty began her journalism in junior high school by writing for her school newspaper. She continued to pursue her interest in journalism in high school and even started a campus magazine with a male classmate. The magazine project taught her some life lessons that planted the seeds for her later writings as a feminist. When her male co-editor told her that he would like to be her best friend if only she were a boy, Betty began to discern the limits that society placed on men and women in the 1930s. To her, it was unfortunate that society would accept her as a boy's girlfriend but not as his close platonic friend. Though Betty did not realize it yet, she would dedicate much of her adult life to challenging and changing these narrowly circumscribed gender roles.

In 1938 at the age of seventeen, Betty graduated from Peoria High School as one of six valedictorians. She then continued her education at Smith College, a prestigious women's college in Massachusetts. There, Betty's gained an increased pride in being a woman. Over the next four years, she developed an interest in psychology and chose it as her major. Betty excelled in her studies, developed her writing ability, and graduated with honors (summa cum laude) in 1942 with a degree in psychology.

After graduation, she moved to the west coast in 1943 to attend the University of California Berkeley. After her first year of graduate study there, she was awarded a prestigious fellowship to get her Ph.D. Her relationship with first serious boyfriend, however, placed her in a difficult dilemma. Her boyfriend was a graduate student who had not been offered a similarly generous fellowship. He threatened to end the relationship unless Betty rejected her fellowship. As she later said, she ultimately decided to turn down the fellowship because she feared herself ending up as a spinster or an "old maid college teacher." She noted that at Smith College, there were few female professors who had husbands and children. Regarding her rejection of a potential career in psychology, she later wrote in 1963, "I never could explain, hardly knew myself, why." This was an important step in how *The Feminine Mystique* came to be written.

After turning down her fellowship, Betty moved to New York City in 1944 to be a reporter for a workers' newspaper. That year, the U.S. had just entered World War II, and with so many men sent off to war, ample job opportunities were available for women in the city. Betty gained valuable experience working as a journalist for the *Workers' Press*. Covering strikes and labor disputes, Betty learned about discrimination in the work-place. It came not just from employers, but employees and unions.

As a staff writer for the Federated Press, a politically liberal news service, Betty wrote articles in support of African Americans and union members. She also criti-cized reactionary forces that, in her view, were working secretly to undermine progressive social advances. At Federated Press, Betty also gave attention to women's problems. Soon after she began working there, she interviewed Ruth Young, one of the clearest voices in the labor movement articulating women's issues. In the resulting article, Betty pointed out that the government could not solve the problem of turnover "merely by pinning up thousands of glamorous posters designed to lure more women into industry." Neither women, nor unions, nor management, she quoted Young as saying, could solve problems of escalating prices or inadequate child care that were made even more difficult by the fact that "women still have two jobs to do." The action of the federal government, Betty wrote, was needed to solve the problems working women faced. Betty also paid special attention to stories about protecting the jobs and improving the situation of workingwomen, including married ones with children.

At the time Betty was a journalist, women were paid a fraction of what men earned doing the same job, and when men returned from the war, women were fired without warning or compensation. Even worse, women who belonged to labor unions were not taken seriously by labor leaders. Their complaints were rarely heard and the unions seldom did anything to help them gain fair pay or get their jobs back.

While Betty reported for the Workers' Press, she became very politically active in New York. She attended rallies to end the war and helped arrange illegal abortions for women she met in college and at work. In 1947 she met Carl Friedan. They fell in love, married, and had their first son shortly thereafter. (Eventually, the two would encounter problems in their marriage and would finally divorce in 1969.)

Betty continued as a reporter for the Workers' Press until 1949 when she became pregnant with her second son. When she asked for a second maternity leave, she was fired. At the time, such treatment of pregnant women was the norm. Men could have careers and families, but it was nearly impossible for women to have both. Again, as with her high school magazine editing experience, Betty was faced with an either-or choice. She responded by leaving her career to become a full-time wife and mother. The family soon moved to the suburbs, where a third child was born.

She devoted most of the next decade living as a homemaker, the life she had been taught would make her the most happy as a woman, Betty realized that she nevertheless felt incomplete and as a result she began to develop a theory on women. It concerned the dangers of what she saw as a myth: the idea that women should be completely satisfied with their roles as wives and mothers and that it was abnormal to want a career or an identity separate from the family. Betty was curious to know if other women felt the same way and began questioning her friends and other women. In 1956, she started down the path that would lead to her first book, *The Feminine Mystique*, as she read over the responses of her college classmates to a questionnaire in anticipation of their fifteenth reunion in 1957. When Betty read the responses to her questionnaire, she felt both panicked and relieved. To her astonishment, Betty found she was not alone in her dissatisfaction. Most of her classmates, who had also given up their careers to become full-time wives and mothers, responded that they too felt incomplete; some were even deeply depressed. It was comforting to know that she was not alone in her views but, at the same time, it was greatly disturbing to learn that so many women were so unhappy. Told that they should be wholly satisfied living their lives for their husbands and children, Betty and her classmates felt guilty for wanting more out of life. It was not that they wished to give up their families. They simply wanted to use their minds for more than just completing mundane household tasks. They wanted careers as well as families. Few women, however, were willing to admit that out loud in 1956.

At this point, Betty knew that she had to be a writer. She realized that the Smith professors were probably indicative of a wider problem. She realized that there was something here which her suburban peers could not fully articulate. Yet this "Problem That Has No Name" was a national epidemic.

Betty organized her data into an article and submitted it to several national women's magazines. One by one, the male editors who controlled *The Ladies' Home Journal, McCall's*, and other leading publications rejected the article, saying that her idea was crazy and that only "sick" women could possibly feel dissatisfied being full-time wives and mothers. By this time, however, Betty knew otherwise and set out to turn her article into a book.

For the next five years, Betty worked on her book while her children were at school. Using her well-developed research skills, she conducted interviews and began a series of studies with women across the nation. She gathered information on everything from the history of women's struggle for voting rights in the U.S. to the rate at which college graduates had children during the 1940s and 1950s. Just as she suspected, Betty found that the Smith graduates were not alone in their feelings, and by 1963 she came up with a label for the silent suffering that millions of women were experiencing. She called it "the feminine mystique." In essence, her book's thesis was that women were victims of a pervasive system of delusional and false values that urged them to find their fulfillment and identity vicariously through their husbands and children.

Many people, however, were not ready to hear what Betty had to say. First, her agent refused to handle the book, and when she found a publisher on her own, the company would only issue a few thousand copies. Many were not willing to admit that a feminine mystique existed, and Friedan's agent and publisher thought most men and women would feel threatened by the book's main idea. Once the book was published in 1963, however, support for it was far greater than expected. By 1966 more than three million copies had been sold. It had become an immediate and controversial best-seller.

The Feminine Mystique today is regarded as one of the most influential American books of the twentieth century and a catalytic work of the women's movement.

What made the book so popular was that Betty told a compelling personal story about her own career choices. Her personal story resonated with the experiences of many of her readers. It seemed that the "strange stirring ... sense of dissatisfaction" that Betty and her college friends felt was common. The feminine mystique, which told women they should be completely content, sacrificing their own dreams for their families, appeared to be taking its toll on millions of American women. In her book, Betty showed that suburban housewives from California to Maine were suffering from a sense of emptiness. Though many were living the female American Dream by going to college and raising a family, they felt incomplete and even obsolete, or used up, once their children were grown.

Friedan maintained that women's unhappiness stemmed from a society, which "does not permit women to accept or gratify their basic need to grow and fulfill their potentialities as human beings." She advocated a "new life plan" that would allow women to have both families and careers and would give them the respect and compensation they deserved for being full-time wives and mothers.

Some notable quotes from The Feminine Mystique include:

The feminine mystique has succeeded in burying millions of American women alive.

It is easier to live through someone else than to become complete yourself.

A girl should not expect special privileges because of her sex but neither should she adjust to prejudice and discrimination.

The problem that has no name—which is simply the fact that American women are kept from growing to their full human capacities—is taking a far greater toll on the physical and mental health of our country than any known disease.

Each suburban wife struggled with it alone. As she made the beds, shopped for groceries, matched slipcover material, ate peanut butter sandwiches with her children, chauffeured Cub Scouts and Brownies, lay beside her husband at night—she was afraid to ask even of herself the silent question—"Is this all?"

Men weren't really the enemy—they were fellow victims suffering from an outmoded masculine mystique that made them feel unnecessarily inadequate when there were no bears to kill.

If divorce has increased by one thousand percent, don't blame the women's movement. Blame the obsolete sex roles on which our marriages were based.

Although she had never planned to start a revolution, Betty had launched the women's liberation movement with her publication of *The Feminine Mystique*. Not surprisingly, Betty was immediately cast as the leader of movement. Letters of support from women throughout the nation began pouring in, with most saying that the book drastically changed their lives.

Betty took her new leadership role very seriously. She began lecturing throughout the country, explaining her ideas for change, and dispelling the myth that women should be totally satisfied being wives and mothers. She wanted people to know that women could find happiness in non-family-related careers. She also wanted more than to just criticize the current climate in which women lived; she wanted to offer real solutions that could be applied quickly and relatively easily. She advocated professional training and shared jobs, where two women share the same position and split the hours of work. This would accommodate the millions of mothers who wanted to work and spend time with their children. She called for day care centers to be set up at or near offices and paternity leave for men as well as women so that both parents could share in early childhood experiences without having to sacrifice their careers.

Betty was a pioneer in her efforts to reinvent America's institutions. She became one of the first of her era to call for ratifying the Equal Rights Amendment, which would outlaw sex discrimination in the Constitution.

As Betty toured the country advocating her ideas, she began to realize that women needed a national organization to promote their interests. Inspired by the civil rights movement, which had just succeeded in getting the Civil Rights Act of 1964 passed, she met with women in Washington, D.C., to discuss starting "an NAACP for women". In June, 1966, at the Washington Hilton Hotel, Friedan and several others, including Kay Clarenbach of the Women's Bureau, Dorothy Haener of the United Auto Workers union, and Muriel Fox, a top public relations expert, wrote out on a napkin the first major structure of the women's movement. They set out to take the actions needed to bring women into the mainstream of American society "now" and to obtain full equality for women in fully equal partnership with men. That message on a napkin became the cornerstone of the National Organization for Women (NOW), which was officially launched a few months later on October 29, 1966.

Betty became NOW's first president, a post she held through 1970. Clarenbach was named chairman of the board, and Richard Graham, head of the Equal Employment Opportunity Commission, was named vice president.

NOW did not have an official office but was run out of various members' homes and workplaces. Mailings were sent out of the United Auto Workers building in Detroit, public relations was handled through Fox's office, and NOW headquarters were located at Betty's apartment on West 72nd Street in New York City.

Under Betty's presidency, NOW concentrated on enacting Title VII of the Civil Rights Act of 1964, which outlawed discrimination on the basis of race or sex. This provision, though passed in 1964, was never enforced by the Justice and Labor Departments and was scoffed at by employers, who continued to advertise "men only" job opportunities. Betty made it NOW's mission to see Title VII enforced and to get women equal pay for equal work, since they were paid sixty cents for every dollar men earned. She also directed activities for legalizing abortion and making birth control widely available. In 1970 Betty led a march of 20,000 women through Washington, D.C., to promote these reforms.

By the 1970s, NOW was making significant strides in its campaign for equality. Title VII was beginning to be enforced throughout the country; women were being admitted to more and more professional schools formerly restricted to men only; and rapid changes were occurring in the workplace (which began to adopt shared jobs and to guarantee maternity leave). Betty had come a long way from the day when she was fired for being pregnant. She was now acting to make American society a land of equal opportunity for all its citizens, male and female, whether they could chose professional careers, domestic careers, or both.

From 1970 to 1973, as the women's movement reached its peak, Betty turned her attention to the women who were not yet fully on board. She, unlike others in the movement, wanted to include even the doubtful home-makers in the struggle for equality, which she considered the reason for all human revolution and for American democracy.

Calling it a human rights movement, Betty reached out to men and to women through her column in *Mc-Call's* magazine entitled "Friedan's Notebook." In the monthly report, she explained that the women's movement was not a threat to motherhood and that men and women both profited from female equality. She wrote: "Some worry that we'll lose our femininity and our men if we get equality. Since femininity is being a woman and feeling good about it, clearly the better you feel about being yourself as a person, the better you feel about being a woman. And, it seems to me, the better you are able to love a man." Betty's columns reached eight million readers and had a profound impact on mainstream society.

In 1970 Betty resigned the presidency of NOW to concentrate on political reform, teaching, and writing. As a founding member of the National Women's Political Caucus in 1971, she was a leader of the campaign for the ratification of the Equal Rights Amendment. In 1973, she helped coordinate the International Feminist Congress and the First Women's Bank.

During this time, she was finding herself increasingly at odds with some other women's "lib" leaders who, she felt, were promoting "female chauvinism" (the opposite of male chauvinism), in which women considered men to be second-class citizens. She saw these leaders as endangering the progress of the women's movement. Betty felt women's liberation should be about choices and equality of opportunity and should include all who believed in those ideals.

She defined feminism as a woman's right to "move in society with all the privileges and opportunities and responsibilities that are their human and American right. This does not mean class warfare against men, nor does it mean the elimination of children." Betty thought that some leaders were anti motherhood and anti man, and she feared that if the women's movement were defined in those terms it would surely fail.

In 1975 Betty Friedan was named Humanist of the Year. Through the 1970s, 1980s, and into the 1990s, she taught in various universities and campaigned vigorously on women's issues. She also wrote three additional books since the publication of *The Feminine Mystique*. In 1981, she wrote *The Second Stage*, which assessed the status of the women's movement. *The Fountain of Age*, published in 1993, addresses the psychology of old age and seeks to counter the notion that aging means loss and depletion. Her memoir, *Life So Far*, appeared in 2000.

Today, in the twenty-first century, she continues to write, lecture, and teach. In 1981, thinking about the movement she had done so much to create, Friedan wrote: "There is no question today that women feel differently now about themselves than they did twenty years ago ... It has been great for women to take themselves seriously as people, to feel some self-respect as people, to feel that they do have some equality even though we know it has not been completely achieved ... We're only beginning to know what we're capable of."

Sources

Information contained in this chapter was excerpted, quoted, and/or paraphrased from:

http://speakers.com/bfriedan.html

http://www.historicpeoria.com/select.cfm?chose=115

http://www.americanwriters.org/writers/friedan.asp

http://muse.jhu.edu/demo/american_quarterly/
48.1horowitz.html

http://www.theatlantic.com/issues/99sep/9909friedan.htm

http://womenshistory.about.com/library/qu/blqufrie.htm

http://www.edc.org/WomensEquity/women/friedan.htm

http://www.assumption.edu/dept/history/Hi113net/
Betty%20Friedan

GLORIA STEINEM:
THE FOUNDER OF
MS. MAGAZINE

A S A JOURNALIST AND feminist leader, Gloria
Steinem has been a leader in the late twentieth
century women's rights movement. Her most well
known accomplishment is the founding of *Ms.* magazine,
the first national women's magazine run by women.

Gloria had an unusual childhood. Her mother suffered
from a psychological illness and her father worked as a
traveling antiques dealer and small-time resort operator.
Home life for Gloria was not stable, and her father left
the family in 1944 when she was ten years old.

After Gloria's sister left home for college, Gloria was
handed the responsibility of taking care of her ill mother.
In her senior year of high school, Gloria's moved in with
her sister in Washington, D.C. With the pressure of caring
for her mother lifted, Gloria flourished. She was elected
vice president of her high school graduating class and
was accepted to Smith College. There, Gloria majored
in government and became politically active on campus.
She even volunteered for Adlai Stevenson's presidential
campaign.

While in college, Gloria learned that her mother's
mother had been a suffragette. Her mother had also

been a very successful columnist and editor, but had to relinquish her career when she married. As was typical of the time, she could not have both a career and a family simultaneously and consequently she suffered from depression. For Gloria, this demonstrated the extreme dangers of restricting women.

Gloria graduated from Smith in 1956 and accepted a Fellowship to study in India for two years. On the way there, she stopped in England for the summer. While there, she discovered that she was pregnant. The father was her former boyfriend. She could return to the U.S., marry, have the baby, and thereby give up her career and education just as her mother had done. Or, she could fulfill the dreams her mother had not been able to realize. Gloria chose the latter choice and had an abortion. Because of the tremendous pain and shame she felt, she would not mention the abortion to anyone for another fifteen years.

After two years of study and activism in India, Gloria returned to the United States. Unfortunately, when she arrived in New York, she discovered that few women were being hired as reporters, and therefore she could not find a job. After two years, however, she finally landed a job with *Help!* magazine. She also began freelance writing and by 1963 she was earning enough to embark on a full-time career as a freelancer.

Though Gloria's career was on the rise, she still was not getting any serious political assignments, such as reporting on presidential candidates. Instead, her male magazine editors assigned her celebrity interviews and even suggested that she go undercover as a *Playboy* bunny.

For the next five years, Gloria freelanced and continued to push for political assignments. Finally in 1968, after building up her career as a freelancer, Gloria was finally able to land an assignment covering George McGovern's presidential campaign. That assignment led to a position as a founding editor at *New York* magazine.

As an editor and political columnist for New York magazine, Gloria covered everything from the assassination of Martin Luther King, Jr., to the United Farm Workers demonstrations led by Caesar Chavez. She did more than just report on the events. She also marched, spoke, and helped to raise money for the causes she backed. Her work and political activity taught Gloria to organize effectively. At first she was not sure why she felt so strongly about working for the oppressed, but then, while attending abortion hearings in 1969, it became clear. As she later wrote: "I finally understood why I identify with 'out' groups. I belong to one too."

Gloria realized that women were oppressed as a class and that she had much in common with the millions of other women who had also had abortions. This was a jolting realization and a pivotal moment in Gloria's life. She had not before realized that such a majority of women felt oppressed by society and that so many had suffered because of restrictive government policies on abortion and other issues. By now Gloria was skilled in political organizing and she turned her energies to advocating for women's rights.

Gloria shifted to exploring the women's liberation movement and explaining the theories of "new feminism" to a broad audience. Through her research, Gloria discovered that the women's liberation movement appeared to be geared only towards older white women. Gloria decided that she would serve as a "bridge" between the generations and unite women of color to help build a broaden base of support for women's rights.

True to her ideals, she marched with thousands of generationally and racially diverse women in the New York City Women's Strike For Equality and began a friendship with Dorothy Pitman Hughes, an African American activist. Hughes encouraged Gloria to speak publicly to promote women's equality, and together the two embarked on a speaking tour of the nation. Advocating legalized abortion, equal pay for equal work, and passage of the Equal Rights Amendment, Gloria and Dorothy made a tremendous impact on society. Crossing racial and class lines, they were able to attract support from women and men throughout the nation. The two formed the Women's Action Alliance to develop women's educational programs and in 1971 they laid down the plans to publish their own magazine. Run by women for women, the magazine would serve as a forum for feminist issues. Gloria and Dorothy gave the publication the title *Ms.* and the first issue went into circulation in January 1972.

In 1972, with the country locked in heated debate over whether or not abortion should be legal, Gloria announced publicly that she was one of the millions of American women who had an illegal abortion. She called on the Supreme Court and federal government to make the choice legal. Due to Gloria's strong personal stand and those of other women who had been through her same dilemma, public sentiment leaned "pro choice." In 1973, the Supreme Court legalized abortion in the landmark case Roe v. Wade.

Gloria has been a founder of several organizations, including the Ms. Foundation for Women, the National

Women's Political Caucus (a nonpartisan organization that promotes pro equality women candidates), and the Coalition of Labor Union Women. In 1975 she helped plan the women's agenda for the Democratic National Convention, and she continued to exert pressure on liberal politicians on behalf of women's concerns. In the fall of 1993, she was inducted into the National Women's Hall of Fame in Seneca Falls, New York.

Since the height of the women's liberation movement, Gloria has continued to write, speak, and contribute to *Ms.* magazine. In her books, Gloria has argued for the causes that occupied her energies for the past four decades. She continues to call for an end to women's disadvantaged condition in the paid labor force, for the elimination of sexual exploitation, and for the achievement of true equality of the sexes.

In 2000, Gloria, who once dismissed marriage as an institution that destroys relationships, married for the first time at the age of 66.

Sources:

The information in this chapter was excerpted from the follow Web sites:

http://www.theglassceiling.com/biographies/bio32.htm

http://abcnews.go.com/sections/us/DailyNews/
steinem000906.html

THE FEMINIST AGENDA AND
THE CIVIL RIGHTS MOVEMENT

I N 1980 IN CHICAGO, 90,000 individuals came together to demand the passage of the Equal Rights
Amendment. The women were having difficulty
in counteracting the right wing Republicans who were
successfully influencing their party to come out strongly
against the ERA. Many Republican moderate women
were working together with other pro ERA supporters,
including the former First Lady Betty Ford. Although it
had seemed that ERA was unstoppable, it was defeated.
A major factor for its defeat was Phyllis Schlafly, who
urged conservatives to mobilize if they wanted to prevent
the drafting of eighteen-year-old girls, federal funds for
abortion, and legislation granting gay and lesbian equal
rights. Schlafly strategies and tactics worked, with the
help of President Reagan and his supporters.

The goals of the 1980s movement were the same as
those of the 1970s. The hallmark of both periods was
a continuing demand for female economic and political
empowerment. The consequences of Reagan's measures
against the ERA were especially disastrous for poor
women. The Republicans' and conservatives' public
outcry about divorced women and welfare mothers did
not bring any solutions to the table. In fact, the women

who were most victimized were blamed for having the problems created by their victimization. Reagan also succeeded as well in reducing AFDC recipient benefits. The end result was that everyone paid more tax except for the rich. The greatest irony in the U.S. in the1980s and 1990s was the emotions that were generated against AFDC. In addition to creating the backlash against AFDC recipients, this period was known by the escalating violence of anti-gay anti-abortion campaigners. The issue of control over reproduction brought about many attacks on Planned Parenthood clinics and violent picketing around the clinics. In counter-action to these anti-abortion campaigns, the pro-choice movement mobilized masses of sympathizers to their cause.

In the United States and around the world, women were becoming cognizant of the fact that the challenge to dominant economic values and the true meaning of human rights was a global struggle. This struggle for equality was especially necessary in poor countries in Asia, Africa, and Latin America, as well as women in developed and richer countries. The gathering of women activists at Beijing, China, in the fall of 1995 was a long-awaited sign for the development of a global networking system among all women. Similar problems plagued women all over the world—rape, domestic violence, exploitation were just some of these.

WOMEN LEAD THE STRUGGLE FOR PROGRESS ON MANY FRONTS

THE ADVERTISING SLOGANS THAT tell women they "have it all" are false. Women were told they had it all in the 1920s, as well as 1950s, 1960s, and the 1980s. It is important to have a full understanding of the past and how it made the historical forces at play today.

Abortion opponents and others who want to have control over women and their reproductive rights are working hard not just to outlaw abortion but to criminalize it. Women around the world are dying from illegal abortions and in many places they have been convicted of murder and are serving long sentences for having abortions. If the "pro life" campaign succeeds in making abortion illegal in the U.S., many women will die from illegal abortion. And many more will have children they do not want or cannot support.

A belief in female inferiority is pervasive in many countries. Many countries today, including the United States, continue ardent attempts to regulate and control women, despite feminist efforts to raise awareness of the injustice continuously perpetuated against women.

Nineteenth century scientists and philosophers in European countries devoted considerable time to producing theories and proofs that proclaimed the inherent inferiority of women and people of color. These same scientists introduced evidence based on physiognomy and special intelligence tests that all groups were subjected to, with the exception of white gentile males. The works of those men provided a "scientific" base for fascism, justifying even the white genocidal practices in Africa. These theories are responsible for all other sexist and racist ideologies in the West.

Refusal to see women as full human beings is a contributing factor in domestic violence against women. Judges impose longer sentences on women who commit crimes, and during the incarceration of women they are treated much more harshly than men. There are still lawyers and judges who do not take sexual assault seriously when the victim and the accused know each other. Women typically receive more time in prison for illegal possession of weapons than men convicted of murder.

In all societies policies are made to control women economically, sexually, and legally. Many people even today believe that a man's main job is to support a family and that women work only to buy more of life's luxuries. In reality, of course, most women work to pay for their children and household expenses. American businesses today not only fail to supply childcare facilities, they don't even acknowledge the need for it.

From early childhood, males are bombarded with messages that "real" men dominate women and control their behavior and verbal and physical abuse of women is viewed as permissible. All these attitudes are evident in many video games that young adults and teenagers watch for hours every day.

Physical force to subjugate females exists throughout the world. Male violence toward women could not be pandemic around the world—including the United States—without the cooperation of the entire social system and its governing institutions. Systemic oppression of women would not continue without the cooperation of individual men and this oppression would not be possible without the cooperation of the whole social system, its police, legislators, and welfare agencies.

Many men continue to expect women to take major responsibility for maintaining all of their needs. This desire and expectation comes from infancy. On the other hand some women perpetuate the system as well out of habit and fear that if they do not take care of men they will be alone. They do not seem to understand that no amount of quality care and service will keep men from being violent toward women.

The images of femininity as well as the images of masculinity are social creations, more than the natural law of order. New historical perspectives continue to emerge and women's activism on the left and on the right will stand in direct contradiction of the prevailing myth of women's passivity.

The full extent of what women have accomplished in this century did not really become self evident until the 1960s. This was when women all over the world became part of a second wave of women's liberation. Women were looking for answers that could not be found in books and publications. Even by the 1960s, women's history was still not easy to ferret out.

It was apparent, however, that there was a strong connection between women's history in the United States and Britain. This is because suffrage campaigns, peace movements, unions and birth control were often connected in the two countries.

The period between 1900 and 1930 saw many forms of social welfare organizing. Through books, movements of people, popular culture, and mass media, the destinies of the two societies were also linked in the period between World War I and World War II.

But much of the movement for self-realization for both nations had common roots in New York's bohemian Greenwich Village. Here feminists gathered to discuss women's role in the culture and politics of American society. The anarchist Emma Goldman had been discussing issues of free love and birth control in her magazine *Mother Earth* as early as 1906.

Charlotte Perkins Gilman, the socialist feminist and thinker, was writing about women's economic dependence as early as the end of the nineteenth century. Gilman and Goldman were in contact with rebels of all persuasions who came together to discuss politics, arts, philosophy, and their personal life stories.

In 1912, Mary Jenny Howe, a suffrage campaigner, formed a heterodoxy club where the first debates on feminism and gender relations took place. Many immigrants to America kept in touch with events and progressive ideas from their respective native countries. Radical ideas crossed the Atlantic Ocean via journals and other printed materials. News of women's social and political unions also reached the American activists. The daughter of Katie Stanton, Harriet Stanton Beach, formed the Equality League of Self Supporting Women in New

York after returning from Britain in 1907. The Equality League vied for an alliance with the Women's Trade Union League, thus integrating political demands with the economic conditions of working women.

In 1909, Clara Leimlich appeared in the front of a strike meeting in New York's Cooper Union Hall, called by the International Ladies Garment Workers Union (ILGWU), and demanded a general strike. Leimlich, a Jewish immigrant from Russia, had studied Marxist theory at the Rand School, an institute for workers that was started by the American Socialist Party. The strikers were not successful in getting all of their demands, but employers from larger and more modern factories were willing to negotiate with the ILGWU. Subsequently, a wave of strikes in the garment industry in Rochester, Chicago, Philadelphia, and Cleveland, took place. Women demanded better pay and better working conditions. Between 1905 and 1915, close to one hundred thousand workers in the clothing industry were involved in labor disputes and by 1919 more than half of women working in the clothing industry were unionized.

The Women's Trade Union League and the Industrial Workers of the World, under the leadership of Emma Goldman and Mother Jones, made common cause. The two unions WTUL and IWW were one during the garment strike of 1911 in Chicago. Community women helped union women by providing food and accommodations for 50,000 people a day. The League persuaded landlords to wait for payment from the striking workers and not to evict them. Some women attacked scabs with red pepper. Others humiliated soldiers in any way they could. The IWW's members also received support from radical middle class women, many outside of Chicago.

A young nurse active in the Socialist Party, Margaret Sanger, took many children under her wing to New York where she found sympathetic families to take them in.

Not only that, women in other industries were forming unions. The telephone operators were demanding eight-hour workdays, two weeks paid vacation, and automatic pay increases. Women trade unionists and social reformists put pressure on states to prevent exploitation. Under pressure from Florence Kelley, a leading personality in the National Consumers League, a number of states passed legislation to protect women and children by demanding the improvement of working conditions at workplaces. Middle class reformers were responsible for the creation of the National Child Labor Committee for protective legislation against child exploitation and employment.

The depression from 1907 to 1908 resulted in widespread unemployment and women, armed only with brooms, resisted eviction collectively. The tenement buildings in which they lived had very few bathrooms. There was a big discrepancy in living conditions between rural and urban poor and the middle class.

By the early 1910s, young middle-class women were entering the higher education system and the labor force in large numbers. This alarmed many people. American commentators were worried by what they considered a generational crisis of authority in the middle class. And they complained about the divorce rate, women's loss of femininity, and the rebellion of children against their parents.

This did not stop the radical women of the time committed to disseminating information about sex and birth control. What is for certain, these activities were in conflict with those who called themselves of guardians of virtue.

U.S. Post Office Inspector Anthony Comstock was very concerned about "immoral literature." When Margaret Sanger wrote an article "What Every Girl Should Know" in a socialist magazine, that issue was banned by the post office under the Comstock Law of 1912. This no doubt persuaded Sanger to make the spreading of information about contraception her life's work. Influenced by ideas of workers' control then making the rounds in syndicalist and socialist circles, Sanger came up with the term "birth control." Sanger first used the term in her magazine, *The Woman Rebel*.

World War I was the time of division among women activists, some of whom supported President Woodrow Wilson's decision to go to war and those who opposed it. Even the respectable members of the American Union Against Militarism were turning towards war work. Only a small number of socialists and Industrial Workers of the World, also known as "Wobblies," abstained from direct involvement. The IWW did not oppose the war, but they refused to accept Woodrow Wilson's strike ban and for that thousands of them were arrested.

Mary Church Terrell, the distinguished black writer and lecturer, chose patriotism and applied for a clerical post in the War Department. Although Terrrell wanted to help war efforts, and appealed to the director, she was told she wouldn't be hired because black people have questionable morals. Still, Terrell never gave up her struggle for the collective improvement of black Americans. Terrell was cofounder of the Women Wage Earners' Association. In 1917, in Norfolk, Virginia, hundreds of black women—domestics, nurses, waitresses,

and tobacco workers—demanded higher wages and hu-
mane working conditions. Joining the women were some
men, the oyster shuckers. Their claim for better wages
was considered an illegal sabotage. Police were brought
in and used wartime legislation to arrest the strikers.

By 1914, the American suffrage movement grew state
by state. Alice Paul advocated a more militant confron-
tational tactic to demand a federal amendment on the
issue of women's voting.

While progressive women activists demanded a new
kind of womanhood based on freedom and equality,
the opponents of women's didn't share their vision.
Congressmen openly mocked women's involvement in
partisan politics and said women should be satisfied with
their own private estates as queen of the American home.
Simultaneously, two strong women's movements developed side by side—one was based on suffrage and the
other was based on peace.

Early in 1915, the Women's Peace Party was established by Jane Addams and Lillian Wald. The National
Women Party organized an International Congress of
Women at The Hague in April, 1915, where thousands
of representatives from twelve countries came seeking to
prevent war and to gain the right to vote. With a common bond as mothers, the participants of the conference
formed the Women's International League for Peace and
Freedom (WILPF).

Crystal Eastman challenged the political mainstream
and worked with the American Union Against Militarism (AUAM), which later became the Civil Liberties Bureau. In 1916, AUAM, under the leadership of Eastman
and trade unionists from the American Federation of
Labor (AFL), met with Mexican labor unions. The two

countries were at the brink of war. Influenced by labor unionists, President W. Wilson appointed a peace commission and the war was prevented. Eastman believed it was possible to democratize international relations: "We must make it known to everybody that people acting directly, not through their governments or diplomats or armies, stopped that war and can stop all wars if enough of them will act together and act quickly."

Although many activists answered the call for war, Crystal Eastman was true to her anti-war stand. She demanded liberty of conscience for Americans against the war. The Espionage Act of June 1915, made speaking and organizing against war an offense punishable by up to twenty years in prison. The Women's Peace Party was forced to close its newsletter *Four Lights* and the party stopped all their anti-war agitation as well. However, Emma Goldman continued her anti-war agitation and was imprisoned for two years and was fined of $10,000. NAWSA did not lose its pacifist stance, however.

Carrie Chapman Catt was a loyal supporter of the war effort, but she continued to question President Wilson's fight for democracy because it deprived patriotic middle-class women and working class women of their right to vote. Catt's approach paid off when Congresswoman Jeannette Rankin introduced a suffrage amendment into Congress in January, 1918. It passed with a one-vote margin.

The Women's Trade Union League provided a crucial connection between the working-class and the campaign for franchise. By recruiting working class women for suffrage parades, it proved that suffrage supporters were women from many backgrounds—homemakers, mothers, teachers, and daughters. This collective participation of many women proved that workingwomen were not the undersexed freaks that anti suffragists were declaring them to be. The recruitment of working women paid off and it had a positive impact on male voters as well. Working class women were becoming increasingly active in the suffrage movement because they wanted political power and labor reforms.

The outbreak of World War I did bring limited state intervention in the industrial sector and some WTUL members were appointed to labor regulation positions. The textile and clothing factories where the majority of women were employed were regulated by the Board of Protocol Standards from 1913. When the United States entered the war, women were gradually replacing men in the workplace, but trade unions, which had been male dominated, were having trouble accepting this. By 1918 there were millions of women working in steel and lumber mills, repairing railway tracks, working as streetcar conductors, and delivering mail.

The jobs women got often depended on their ethnic and racial backgrounds. Black women were leaving domestic work and going to work in manufacturing jobs. Jewish and European women worked in ammunition plants. But black women encountered much harsher working conditions and they had the worst of the jobs and the lowest paying jobs. They were segregated, which usually meant their working conditions were particularly bad.

Mary Church Terrell worked very hard to combat the segregation laws. However, the Southerners around President Wilson lobbied successfully to enforce segregation in governmental jobs. Thousands of African Americans from the South migrated up north in search of work.

Women who were forced to work for white families in the rural South could be coerced back to work based on vagrancy laws. However, in spite of the obstacles, women followed and sometimes even led the trek to northern cities.

Before World War I, control over fertility and birth control were still dangerous subjects and punishable by law. In 1914, federal agents came to Margaret Sanger's home and served her with an indictment for violating the Comstock Law in her journal *The Woman Rebel*. She was arraigned in the U.S. district court in New York and had to flee to Montreal from where she left for Europe under an assumed name. She sent a cable authorizing the release of 100,000 copies of her pamphlet "Family Limitation," which gave information about birth control methods. She appealed to distributors to disseminate this information to poor working women and men who were overburdened with large families—there were some men and women who had 16 children.

Margaret made good use of her time in Europe and researched the history and practice of birth control. Sanger's supporters in the United States were mostly linked to the Socialist Party, the Industrial Workers of the World, and some anarchist circles. Grassroots agitation for birth control was also developing in the United States under the auspices of Elizabeth Gurley Flynn, Emma Goldman, and the socialist Kate Richards O'Hare. Birth control activists equated the censoring of information about birth control and fertility to the rights of workers to control their own lives. When Margaret Sanger returned home to the U.S., large crowds of women came to hear her talk about the right to birth control and thousands of women were sending her letters talking about how they were always exhausted from constant child bearing, male violence, and sexual and physical abuse.

Some of the more radical supporters of the right to birth control took direct action by setting up birth control clinics. Margaret Sanger and her sister Ethel Bryne opened a clinic in Brooklyn, New York, in 1916, where they provided immigrant women information about a birth control method called cervical pessaries. Margaret Sanger and her staff were arrested and Sanger was released from prison after serving three months. After her release from prison, Sanger shifted all her focus to legislative reforms.

The suffrage amendment passed in June 1919, and by November 1920, every state had ratified it. For the first time, American women had the right to vote.

But the end of World War I was a big setback for women in the labor force. Women were discarded from industry. The WTUL was helplessly caught between the employers and labor unions that continued to be hostile towards women's employment. In spite of all the protests, WTUL members were not able to defend displaced women workers.

In 1919, general strikes broke out all over the United States as the workers were freed from the wartime no-strike pledge. Workers everywhere demanded better pay, shorter hours, and collective bargaining rights. These strikes were organized by the American Federation of Labor whose leadership had emerged intact from the World War I, unlike the Wobblies who were compelled to give up their militant action when most of their leaders were jailed.

The post World War II period was also a period of returning to normalcy, but with some differences from

World War I. There was also a reaction to the horrors of war, a reaction that penetrated at the heart of great liberal ideas. The period was known as the age of anxiety and in part there was an ever-growing fear of totalitarianism. Liberals tried to redefine their place in American politics as they tried to find the middle road best suited to American democratic ideals. American liberals felt as uneasy about the radical left as the radical right.

After the death of President Roosevelt, Eleanor Roosevelt worried that liberals had to create a new leadership which would further continue the legacy of humanizing social reforms. Mrs. Roosevelt wanted the United States to pursue a more equitable democracy. Until her death, she continually asserted that civil liberties and civil rights were the cornerstone of American democracy and therefore she never stopped campaigning for the civil rights of African American and all other disenfranchised peoples. She venomously opposed the House un-American Activities Committee and Senator Joseph McCarthy's rhetoric in defending his anti-communist witch hunting policy.

There were no notable advances in the two decades after World War II in the fight for women's rights. Groups that had been active earlier entered a state of dormancy, waiting for a force to emerge and reawaken the passion of the feminists of the past. Before the emergence of the civil rights movements of the 1960s, women in the United States and around the world were receiving little respect as a gender and even the heroic efforts of women in the past was given no broad recognition or acknowledgment. The women's liberation movement of the 1960s was a psychological and ideological process that had been gestating for two decades. The women of the movement knew that liberation would not be easy and that it would require extraordinary means to bring it to completion.

A new respect for women seeped through every aspect of society, but still too many women seemed to take their perceived inferiority for granted. Some women began to see a need to identify themselves as women and to connect with each other on a personal level in order to question the stereotypes and protest the treatment that resulted from it.

Women had too long been the victims of conditioning that saw their primary role as serving others and sacrificing themselves in almost all aspects of their lives. Secondly, women remained psychologically vulnerable, so if they acted in their own interest they would be accused of being selfish and uncaring. If women were to gain respect and equality with men, the male behavior and psychology toward women had to be changed. Many women understood that they would have to confront men about their behavior directly if the whole system of women's subservience was ever to crumble. They were determined to end the game playing forever.

The main idea of the movement was that each woman had to decide for herself what she wanted out of her life and then working on making it a reality. The media turned this into a claim that women were trying to become like men. Rather, they were trying to claim their own authenticity.

The groundwork for the revolution had been laid out by Betty Friedan. Men were invited to join the movement only if they were genuinely concerned about social justice and equality for women. Although men were invited to join in, the visionaries and the leaders of that social revolution had to be women. Women saw that it was up to them to remake society if equality of the sexes was ever to be achieved. That equality depended on each person's intellect and experience, not on their gender.

THE WAR AGAINST
WOMEN CONTINUES

MANY INSURGENCIES HAVE CHALLENGED the ruling class since the beginnings of Patriarchy thousands of years ago. However, feminism is the first movement ever to challenge patriarchy itself. Today, women continue to organize and to take on major roles in the battles for world peace and to preserve the environment.

Even today, over seventy percent of young women in the United States do not consider themselves feminists. The major reason is that they have been misinformed about the true meaning of feminism. The enemies of feminism have made it unattractive to most American women. The forces that are trying to undermine feminism are very powerful, but most of the backlash against feminism has been invisible to the public eye.

Women, for instance, think that the advances made over the last 100 years are now securely achieved. The facts show a different story. Beginning with President Reagan and the rise of conservatism in the 1980s, a profoundly anti-feminist movement has been ongoing in the political system. Affirmative action and reproductive choices are directly under attack. The junior President Bush is very much in support of eliminating abortion and criminalizing it. Sex education in the public schools has been directly under attack for the last ten years. Over the last twenty years, our country has been becoming increasingly militaristic. Vast resources are used to wage wars while services for children, women, and the elderly are disappearing.

Our political leaders have created a deficit of trillions of dollars fighting some fifty wars since the end of the Cold War. A more militaristic society produces a society that has more violence against women—and that is true not just in the United States but all over the world

The more militaristic our country becomes, the more violent it becomes as well. Children act more and more violently. Military language, images, and behaviors are being used in video games and movies. This also breeds violence and racism that is anti-feminist and racist. Nowadays, children and young adults watch video games and movies hour after hour. The potential for aggression and violence—especially against women—is increasing on many fronts.

Only by analyzing these newly created militaristic attitudes and behavior can we figure out how to objectively change them. The major purpose of war is to prove the superiority of one group of people over another—and anybody who is soft or kind is not in the right camp.

The defense industry in general is very guilty of creating attitudes that deride women. It is no accident that sexist warfare training employs sexist language. So the new military struggle is all about power and not about preservation of life. Militarism generates its own language in order to diffuse the true meaning of its heinous acts. The horrors of war are downplayed with euphemisms whose job it is to hide the brutality of war. If the public remains ignorant, the public will be complacent and will not protest the actions of the military.

This is what the military wants and so it continues to mislead the public through the use of euphemisms that disguise the carnage that war wreaks. In the last four decades, our military was engaged in many countries around the globe where millions of innocent people lost their lives. Yet, this human tragedy is merely called collateral damage or is never mentioned in the first place. To anyone who read George Orwell's *1984*, this distortion of language is a classic example of the double-talk that characterizes a totalitarian society such as was depicted in Orwell's book. Euphemisms are used because frank language shows the true horror of the military complex in people's lives.

Euphemisms are used by every discipline that attacks and kills humans. The term "collateral damage," for example, means that humans were not the intended targets of attacks, but unfortunately they were in the way of a supposedly important operation. The military people even call some nuclear devices "clean bombs" because they emit less radiation but still have a great potential to kill and destroy. Scientists and military strategists have a whole menu from where to choose words that appear to be non threatening and harmless. For example, the euphemism cookie cutter refers to a model of nuclear attack. Military men do not use the term nuclear bombs. Rather, they call them re-entry vehicles (RVs)! Ads used in magazines meant to reach Air Force procurers, for example, promote weapons called "big sticks" or "penetrators." These terms are loaded with sexual innuendoes that perhaps are meant to amuse the men who purchase them.

Pornography is another major factor contributing to violence and cruelty against women. In the past, pornography generally depicted different sexual acts and was free of sadistic acts. In the last decades pornography has changed and is basically promoting unimaginable depths of violence, hatred, and cruelty to women and children. There are even films that feature lynching, mutilation, and murder of women. These acts apparently bring some men to orgasm.

All pornographic material in some way or another present women as dehumanized and as sexual objects who enjoy pain and humiliation. Women are portrayed as sexual objects who experience pleasure in being raped. There is pornography that shows women tied up, cut up, mutilated, and bruised.

Sadistic violence is not necessarily inherent in men's nature. On the contrary, men are indoctrinated into this behavior by such institutions as the military. Military institutions and governmental bodies more than tolerate male sexual aggression against women. They endorse it, which the infamous navy Tailhook incident revealed.

Without media attention, this would still be going on and women would not be telling their stories. These examples of hatred of women appear in military songs, slogans, and cartoons that explicitly point to violence against women as the measure and symbol of male power.

Violence is a response to fear. Most societies foster violence in the dominant males who rule the world. But by emphasizing violence, they are only teaching men that to avoid their inferiority complexes, they have to exert power. That will make them feel better. This worldwide multi-level assault on women is becoming very extreme and many women around the world are uniting against it. Some men are discussing their own sense of identity and their personal feelings in small groups. Male society is starting to realize that male supremacy may work to its advantage in some ways, but it also prevents them from real development and that, ultimately, affects them in a detrimental way.

Women are organizing and opposing these newfound ways of male domination and oppression of women. In many underdeveloped countries, women are developing powerful organizations to help their people out of economic deprivation. In America, women are organizing in hundreds of groups that oppose war, nuclear power, and issues of toxic waste around the country. This new emerging peace movement is drawing women and men together just like white women and black women joined together to fight KKK in the South. During the Cold War, nuclear disarmament got the attention of many peace activists, especially women. Women were very anxious about the arms race between the U.S. and the Soviet Union and they organized through the "Women's Strike for Peace." The founders of WSP were Dagmar Wilson, Eleanor Garst and Margaret Russell. The WSP protested not only against the buildup of nuclear weapons, but also the policies of McCarthy which created a climate of hysteria. The Women's Strike for Peace built important leadership and was an inspiration for the peace movement.

Through their actions, the WSP was very effective and they were responsible for influencing President Kennedy to sign the limited Test Ban Treaty of 1963 (from which President Bush, Jr. withdrew in 2002).

In 1980, women around the world united for peace and declared to the world that militarism equals sexism.

Women are infusing the peace movement with new energy and vitality. As women have been the major victims of male oppression during both times of wars and peace for the past several millennia, they are now fighting back at every front.

Women are in the forefront of the peace movement everywhere. They are demonstrating and endangering themselves and in some countries men are attacking demonstrating women either by verbal abuse, throwing objects at them, hitting them, and even killing them.

In 1989, Israeli, Palestinian, and European women marched for peace from West to East Jerusalem, where they were confronted violently by state police. Many of these three thousand women who were marching in a non-violent way were kicked, hit with sticks, dragged off by their hair, and sprayed with tear gas.

Although the peace movement did not show much visibility, it has been reawakened by the terrorist attacks of September 11, 2001. Once again, women are leading the way. Most peace organizations are led by women. This reawakened movement is providing hope to many people who are now realizing that the current "war on terrorism" is not going to work. It will merely bring more tragedy that will disproportionately impact women and children at home and around the world.

HATTIE WYATT CARAWAY, THE FIRST WOMAN SENATOR

HATTIE WYATT CARAWAY WAS the first woman ever elected to the U.S. Senate. She was elected as one of the senators representing Arkansas in 1932 after winning a special election to fill the remaining months of her deceased husband's term. Hattie Caraway was reelected to the Senate two more times, and she served in the Senate until 1945. The story of Hattie's path to the Senate began with her birth in Bakerville, Tennessee and graduation from Dickson College in 1896. She married one of her classmates, Thaddeus Horatius Caraway, and afterwards the couple moved to Arkansas. As was typical of the time, Hattie took care of their children and the farm while her husband worked as a lawyer. In 1912, Hattie's husband was elected to Congress.

After women gained suffrage in 1920, Hattie voted, although she never deviated from her role as a homemaker. Her husband was re-elected to the 1926 and 1932 Senate seats. Soon after he was elected for the 1932 Senate seat, however, he unexpectedly died on November 6, 1931. The governor of Arkansas appointed Hattie to fill her deceased husband's Senate seat. She was sworn in and later confirmed in a special election on January 12, 1932.

At that time, she became the first woman ever elected to the U.S. Senate. (One woman, Rebecca Latimer Felton, had previously been appointed by the governor of Georgia in 1922 to be Senator, but her appointment was a courtesy that lasted for just one day.)

Hattie made no speeches on the floor of the Senate and as a result, she earned the nickname "Silent Hattie." She learned much about a legislator's responsibilities from her deceased husband. She took these responsibilities seriously and built a reputation of integrity.

In May 1932, she was invited by the vice president to preside over the Senate for a day. She took advantage of the attention paid to this event by surprising Arkansas politicians with her announcement that she was running for reelection. Joseph T. Robinson and other leaders of the Democratic Party in Arkansas did not support her candidacy and told that she would not win the party's nomination. Hattie, however, sought the assistance of populist Huey Long of Arkansas. He saw her as an ally and he agreed to help her in her campaign. As part of his support, he aided her with a nine-day election tour.

Hattie also garnered the support of the American Federation of Labor. In the end, she defeated her nearest competitor by a two to one vote and was reelected to the Senate.

Upon returning to the Senate, Hattie was a loyal supporter of Huey Long's Share Our Wealth campaign. She was also usually supportive of President Franklin D. Roosevelt and his New Deal legislation. She did remain, however, a prohibitionist and voted with many other southern senators against anti lynching legislation.

In 1933, Hattie became the first woman to chair a senate committee when she became chairwoman of the

Committee on Enrolled Bills. In 1936, her position as the lone woman in the Senate changed when Rose McDonnell Long, widow of Huey Long, was appointed to fill out her husband's term.

Hattie ran for Senator once again in 1938. This time, she was opposed by Congressman John L. McClellan who ran with the slogan, "Arkansas needs another man in the Senate." She was supported by organizations representing women, veterans, and union members, and she ended up winning the seat by eight thousand votes.

In 1943, Hattie co-sponsored an early version of the ERA.

Hattie ran one last time in 1944 and was defeated by Congressman William Fulbright. The following year, she was appointed by President Franklin D. Roosevelt to the Federal Employees' Compensation Commission (1945–1946), and later to the Employees' Compensation Appeals Board (1946–1950). After suffering a stroke in 1950, she resigned and died later that same year.

Sources:

The information found in this section was obtained, quoted, and/or paraphrased from:

www.senate.gov/artandhistory/history/minute/First_Woman_Senator_Appointed.htm

http://www.senate.gov/~lincoln/html/hattaway.html

http://womenshistory.about.com/library/bio/blbio_caraway_hattie.htm

http://www.spartacus.schoolnet.co.uk/USAcarawayH.htm

MARGARET "MAGGIE" KUHN, THE CHAMPION OF SENIOR RIGHTS

MARGARET "MAGGIE" KUHN WAS a charismatic leader who changed the way society views and treats the elderly. After being forced to retire at age 65, she realized the rights of the elderly were being denied when it came to retirement and other issues. In response, Maggie became a founder of the Gray Panthers in Philadelphia in 1971. The organization led the fight for the rights of the elderly, and Maggie remained active as an executive of the organization until her death.

Born in Buffalo, New York in 1905, Maggie obtained her B.A. with honors from Case-Western Reserve University in 1926. During that era, higher education for women was still in its infancy, and women were given two career options, nursing and teaching. Without exception, it was expected that career would be interrupted early on for marriage.

In 1930, Maggie became head of the Professional Department of business girls at the YWCA in Philadelphia. She believed in the Y's philosophy, saying "One of the things I valued most about the Y was its belief in the ability of groups to empower the individual and to change society. Social workers back then called it 'group work.' The idea was that individuals find purpose and meaning through group association."

In 1941, at the beginning of World War II, Maggie became a program coordinator and editor for the YWCA's USO division. After the YWCA's USO division was ended 1948, she became program coordinator for the General Alliance for Unitarian and Other Liberal Christian Women in Boston. In 1950, in order to take care of her ailing parents, she accepted a job near them in Philadelphia as assistant secretary of the Social Education and Action Department at the Presbyterian Church's national headquarters. She recalled that, "In the social action department, my co-workers and I urged churchgoers to take progressive stands on important social issues: desegregation, urban housing, McCarthyism, the Cold War, nuclear arms. We believed that without powerful institutions like the Presbyterian Church advocating reform, many problems would go unsolved."

In 1969, she became a program executive for the Presbyterian Church's Council on Church and Race, and was a member of a subcommittee that dealt with the problems of the elderly. She become interested in the issues facing the elderly when in 1961 she attended the White House Conference on Aging as a church observer.

When Maggie reached retirement age at 65, she was distressed because she did not want to stop working. She had never given retirement much thought. She felt energetic enough to go on for many years and the notion of retiring struck her as ludicrous and depressing.

In 1970, at the age of 65, she met with a group of five of her friends to address the problems of retirees. The group that emerged from this meeting was named the Consultation of Older and Younger Adults for Social Change. After a year, the organization grew to one hundred members. The group was renamed the Gray Panthers in 1972. In 1973, eleven chapters of the Gray Panthers were opened. In 1975, the Gray Panthers held its first national convention in Chicago. The Gray Panthers quickly received public attention and grew as a national organization. In 1990, the Gray Panthers' public policy office opened in Washington, D.C. Maggie described the mission of the Gray Panthers by stating "In the tradition of the women's liberation movement, the common mission of all the Gray Panther groups was consciousness raising. Instead of sexism, we were discovering "ageism the segregation, stereotyping, and stigmatizing of people on the basis of age." Over the years, the Gray Panthers have been involved in grassroots activities that deal with public and governmental policies towards senior citizens.

In 1972, Maggie wrote the book *Get Out There and Do Something About Injustice* and in 1977 she wrote *Maggie Kuhn On Aging*. She was also writer and editor for the church magazine *Social Progress* and advisor for the television series for older persons, "Over Easy." Before her death Maggie wrote an autobiography entitled, *The Life and Times of Maggie Kuhn.*

Maggie had never married and speaking about being a single woman she said, "Many people ask why I never married. My glib response is always 'Sheer luck!' When I look back on my life, I see so many things I could not have done if I had been tied to a husband and children."

Sources:

The information included in this section was obtained, paraphrased, and/or quoted from:

http://www.humanistsofutah.org/humanists/margaretkuhn.htm

http://mtmt.essortment.com/maggiekuhn_rfxw.htm

JEANNETTE RANKIN,
THE FIRST CONGRESSWOMAN

J EANNETTE RANKIN WAS THE first woman to serve in the U.S. Congress, and indeed one of the first women ever in the world to be elected to a major legislative body. This was quite an accomplishment considering that her election to Congress occurred at a time when women in most states in the United States could not even vote. As a lifelong pacifist, she voted against U.S. entry into both World War I and World War II, becoming the only member of Congress to do so. She also led a resistance movement against U.S. involvement in Vietnam.

Jeannette was born on a ranch near Missoula, Montana in 1880. She was the oldest of seven children. Her father, John Rankin, was a rancher and lumber merchant. Her mother, Olive Pickering Rankin, was a schoolteacher. As a child, Jeannette attended public schools in Missoula. She received a biology degree from the University of Montana in 1902. Upon graduation, she taught in schools, completed an apprenticeship as a seamstress, and supported herself by taking in sewing.

Jeannette moved across the country in 1904 to study at the New York School of Philanthropy in New York City. After completing her coursework there, she began practicing as a social worker in Seattle, Washington. She did not particularly enjoy her work, however, and she enrolled in the University of Washington. At this time, the women's suffrage movement was building strength. Jeannette became involved in the state suffrage organization and for five years she campaigned for suffrage in Washington, California, Ohio, and Montana. She served as legislative secretary of the National American Woman Suffrage Association, and the efforts of her and other suffragists finally paid off in 1914 when women in Montana won the right to vote.

Now experienced as a political activist, Jeanette launched her political career. In 1916 she ran as a progressive Republican on a platform that included national women's suffrage, child protection laws, and prohibition. Her campaign was successful and she won a seat in U.S. Congress, becoming the first woman to ever do so. Her election was particularly remarkable because she was a Republican who was voted into office in a Democratic state and because she won despite the reality that most women in the United States could not even vote.

Once in the House, Jeanette helped draft an amendment to give women suffrage and she led a successful floor debate on the issue. The proposed amendment was defeated in the Senate, unfortunately, and the amendment was not enacted until 1919. During her term, she also advocated for women's rights in other ways. For example, she introduced the first bill that would have given women citizenship independent of their husbands, and she supported government sponsorship of prenatal and child-care education for women.

During her term, Jeannette sparked the most controversy around World War I. As a pacifist, Jeannette became embroiled in the debate about whether the U.S. should go to war against Germany. During her campaign, the country was generally isolationist, and most people in the U.S. thought the country should not entangle itself with the affairs of other countries. By 1917, however, this sentiment had changed. President Wilson ended diplomatic relations with Germany, and German battleships had sunk American merchant ships. Wilson called a special session of Congress in April, 1917, and the Senate passed a resolution to go to war. When the House then voted on the issue, Jeanette became one of only fifty-six members of the entire Congress, both House and Senate, who voted against declaring war on Germany.

Jeannette later released a statement in which she explained her vote: "I knew that we were asked to vote for a commercial war, that none of the idealistic hopes would be carried out, and I was aware of the falseness of much of the propaganda. It was easy to stand against the pressure of the militarists, but very difficult to go against the friends and dear ones who felt that I was making a needless sacrifice by voting against the war, since my vote would not be a decisive one ... I said I would listen to those who wanted war and would not vote until the last opportunity and if I could see any reason for going to war I would change it."

Although fifty-five male members of Congress had also voted against declaring war, Jeannette's vote received the most attention. Amid calls for her resignation, several suffragist groups even canceled her speaking engagements.

During World War I, Jeannette promoted Liberty Bonds, which were sold to support the war effort, and she also voted for the draft. She did, however, vote against the Espionage Act, which targeted foreign residents of the United States and suppressed dissent.

Most likely as a result of her 1917 vote against the war, Jeannette was unsuccessful in being re-elected in 1918. More than two decades would pass before she ran for Congress again.

Following her departure from Congress, Jeannette remained active in pacifist issues and women's issues. The year following her departure, she joined Jane Addams as a delegate to the Second International Congress of Women. For the next two decades afterwards, she worked in Washington, D.C. as a lobbyist for various groups, including the Women's Peace Union and the National Council for the Prevention of War.

In 1940 Jeannette made her return to the House by running on an anti-war platform. Back in Congress, she was once again faced with the decision about entering another world war. After the bombing of Pearl Harbor in 1941, she was the only member of Congress to vote against declaring war against Japan. Her anti-war vote provoked outrage and it effectively put an end to her political career. John Kennedy later said of her, "Few members of Congress have ever stood more alone while being true to a higher honor and loyalty."

After leaving politics for the second time, Jeannette dedicated herself to social reform. She was drawn to the work of Mohandas Gandhi and she traveled to India seven times between 1946 and 1971. She returned to the anti-war scene in the 1960s when she organized women to protest against the violence in Indochina. In January 1968, at the age of eighty-eight, she led more than 5,000 women who called themselves the Jeannette Rankin Brigade to Capitol Hill to protest against U.S. involvement in Vietnam.

Rankin considered campaigning for a third term in Congress, but her health began to fail and she died in 1973. She is remembered as a woman who courageously advocated for peace and women's rights.

Sources:

Information in this chapter was obtained, quoted, and/or paraphrased from:

http://www.rankinfoundation.org/story.htm

http://www.galegroup.com/free_resources/whm/bio/rankin.htm

SOME OTHER NOTABLE WOMEN

VIRGINIA APGAR (1909–1974)

She was a surgeon, one of the first women to graduate from Columbia University Medical School. She is best known for devising the Apgar Newborn scoring System which measures pulse, respiration muscle tone, and reflexes. The system ensures that correctable problems don't go undetected. The Apgar Score is now used all over the world.

EMILY GREEN BALCH (1867–1961)

She was a pacifist. She stood for beliefs that were very unpopular in her day and because of her beliefs she was persecuted, jailed and suffered tremendously; in 1946 she was vindicated when she received a Nobel Prize for Peace. She cofounded the International League for Peace and Freedom in Geneva and worked for disarmament and she had high hopes for world peace through the efforts of the United Nations.

CLARA BARTON (1821–1912)

She was an American teacher, nurse and founder of the American Red Cross. She worked as an unpaid nurse during the civil War and delivered First Aid equipment from private donations.

EVANGELINE CORY BOOTH (1865–1950)

She was a social reformer who in 1904 became a leader of the Salvation Army in the United States. Under her leadership the Salvation Army established soup kitchens, hospitals for unwed mothers and emergency disaster relief efforts.

LUCY BURNS (1829–1966)

The suffragist who worked with legendary activist Alice Paul, Burns organized a massive women's suffrage parade on March 3, 1913, in Washington D.C. During President Wilson's inauguration 5000 marchers demanded a Constitutional amendment granting women the right to vote. The amendment was passed and ratified before President Wilson left office.

CARRIE CHAPMAN CATT (1859–1947)

One of the first suffragists who was the co-founder of the National League of Women Voters. At the same time she was a voracious advocate for international peace.

DOROTHY DAY (1897–1980)

Through her book *The Long Loneliness* and her newspaper, *The Catholic Worker*, she exposed the inequality in the American class structure and the American government's appetite for armed aggression.

Mary Dennett (1872–1947)

She was an educator and activist who in 1915 founded the National Birth Control League, the first organization in the country to lobby for liberalization of birth control laws.

LAST WORDS

THE STORIES OF THE legendary women in this book are by no means all the stories there are of the women whose impact on history has been great but not fully understood. Women, for the most part, have not been the writers of history. That's been mostly a male's occupation. But that doesn't mean there isn't a crying need for more of that history to be written—and more, to be lived out in reality, whether it is written or not.

Of course part of the reality is the perception of its existence. You can't say just because women's history is a mostly ignored subject, even among women, it doesn't exist. It exists. But it isn't fully appreciated. This modest volume is an attempt to make people appreciate the role that women have played in the advance of the human condition.

This book is at best only a guide. These are a few of the stories that should be told that haven't been told enough. There are many more untold stories. Many more.

Even more exciting is the prospect that the reader—especially the young reader—will know that they too can write their own stories, by what they do in their own lives.

Hopefully, the stories of the women in this book should prove inspirational. They show that change often comes from one person's vision of how things should be. Perhaps this book will inspire other writers to tell more of the story. And perhaps this book will inspire someone to go out and do and be the kind of women who make history and make change. It is known that people who go out and write often do so because of how something they read affected them. People who go out and excel at something, whether its arts or science or music or politics, often do so because of things they read when they were young.

I hope that the reader has seen in a new light the connection between war and peace. I have tried to show the connection between reactionary fundamentalism and militarism. The sudden pervasiveness of military think in our language is truly horrifying. With a fundamentalist in the White House, for example, the glorification of war has reached an unnatural level. All progressive struggle, be it in civil rights by gender or ethnicity, in education, in science, in the environment, is under enormous attack.

People don't become militaristic because it's inevitable. The outsize machismo that has come to predominate in our politics is an intentional thing, pushed by men who want to make America a fascist state instead of a democracy. Witness the bullyish swagger with which President Bush walks.

The violence of our movies is not accidental. Despite the pious posturing that such movies are made because "that's what people want to see," the sudden upswing in glorifying violence has not occurred because suddenly human nature has become more violent than ever. It has occurred because it benefits the kind of men who make profit from militarism and who ideologically believe in a warrior state. They are in pursuit of a bankrupt ideology that is willing to risk destruction of our species and our planet.

So many unexamined assumptions underlie what is suddenly acceptable in society. A cheap and sensationalistic, monopolized press is part of the problem—a big part. Violence is a part of human history, but it is not the only thing in human history. There is also optimism and hope and dreams. There is progress and science. There is art and love. There still is tenderness and sensualness in human beings—maybe more in women than in men at this point. But it exists. There is still creativity instead of destruction. These are much better things than the glorification of violence.

The battle must be joined if the human species is to endure. And women must become the leaders of the effort. They must bring men along with them!

It is apparent by studying American history that women were always in the forefront of needed reform, and not just reform that immediately affected them. Women played a vanguard role in the abolitionist movement, in the labor movement, in the fight to save the environment so the human species could persevere—in all the things that humanize as opposed to all the things that destroy.

Perhaps the most important role for women was in the peace movement. It was this way in the past—it should be this way in the future, when so obviously the struggle for peace is one that must be waged anew and with great vigor.

Look to women for the answers!

The task will be spearheaded by women, and progressive men will then follow their lead.

RECOMMENDED ORGANIZATIONS TO JOIN

There are hundreds of great organizations that are working hard to promote peace and social justice, and it would be impossible to list them all. The ones listed here are well-established groups, which have Web sites that provide links to the many other groups that could not be mentioned directly here.

Code Pink

733 15th Street, NW #507
Washington, D.C. 20005 Phone: (202) 393-5016 & (310) 827-3046
E-mail: info@codepinkalert.org
Website: http://www.codepink4peace.org/

CODEPINK is a women initiated grassroots peace and social justice movement that seeks positive social change through proactive, creative protest and non-violent direct action. Rejecting the Bush Administration's color-coded security alerts that are based on fear, CODEPINK is a feisty call for women and men to "wage peace." In less than a year, CODEPINK has become a vibrant presence in the peace and social justice movement. Very visible and recognizable simply by wearing pink, CODEPINK has found a niche in the movement by addressing serious issues in a multitude of creative—and sometimes outrageous—ways, always bringing into play the sensibilities of respect, compassion and interconnectedness.

(The information presented above about CodePink is quoted directly from the organization's Web site.)

International Action Center

2489 Mission St., #28; San Francisco, CA 94110

Phone: (415) 821-6545

Fax: (415) 821–5782 E-mail: iac@actionsf.org

Website: http://www.iacenter.org/ Website (San Francisco office): http://www.actionsf.org

International Action Center provides information, activism, and resistance to U.S. militarism, war, and corporate greed. The organization also links itself with struggles against racism and oppression within the United States. International Action Center was founded by Ramsey Clark, former U.S. attorney general.

(The information provided here about International Action Center was paraphrased from the organization's Web site.)

International A.N.S.W.E.R.

National Office:

39 W. 14 St., #206 New York, NY 10011

(212) 633-6646

Washington, D.C. Office:

1247 E St., SE Washington, D.C. 20003

(202) 544-3389

E-mail: info@internationalanswer.org

Website: http://www.internationalanswer.org/

(A.N.S.W.E.R. stands for: Act Now to Stop War & End Racism).

Office of the Americas

8124 West Third Street, Suite 202 Los Angeles, California 90048
Phone: 323–852–9808 Fax: 323–852–0655 E-mail: OOA@igc.org
http://www.officeoftheamericas.org/

The Office of the Americas is a non-profit organization dedicated to furthering the cause of justice and peace in the hemisphere through broad based educational programs. Founded in 1983 in Los Angeles, OOA is a recognized source for documentation and analysis of current events in North America, Mexico, Central America, and South America, including the War on Drugs, human rights, and United States foreign policy. The Office is often called upon to present expert testimony in litigation before the Federal Immigration Court.

(The information about the Office of the Americas was quoted directly from the organization's Web site.)

United Children's Network

5951 Montecito Drive, #5
Palm Springs, CA 92264
Phone: (760) 321–4111
E-mail: annactnow@yahoo.com
Website: annanevenic.org

United Children's Network specializes in helping children. Founded in 1989, this non-profit agency helps needy students in public schools. This help includes one-on-one tutoring, extended daycare, and emergency funds for low income families. The organization also informs the public on important issues such as sexuality, birth control, and peer pressure through guest lectures and films. United Children's Network was founded by one of the authors of this book, Anna Nevenic.

Global Exchange

2017 Mission Street, #303 San Francisco, CA, 94110 Phone: 415.255.7296 Fax: (415) 255.7498

Website: http://www.globalexchange.org/

Global Exchange is an international human rights organization dedicated to promoting political, social and environmental justice globally. Since its founding in 1988, Global Exchange has been working to increase global awareness among the U.S. public while building partnerships around the world.

(The information provided above about Global Exchange was quoted directly from the organization's Web site.)

MoveOn.org

Website: http://www.moveon.org/

MoveOn is working to bring ordinary people back into politics. With a system that today revolves around big money and big media, most citizens are left out. When it becomes clear that our "representatives" don't represent the public, the foundations of democracy are in peril. MoveOn is a catalyst for a new kind of grassroots involvement, supporting busy but concerned citizens in finding their political voice. Our international network of more than 2,000,000 online activists is one of the most effective and responsive outlets for democratic participation available today.

When there is a disconnect between broad public opinion and legislative action, MoveOn builds electronic advocacy groups. Examples of such issues are campaign finance, environmental and energy issues, impeachment, gun safety, and nuclear disarmament. Once a group is assembled, MoveOn provides information and tools to help each individual have the greatest possible impact. During impeachment, MoveOn's grassroots advocates generated more than 250,000 phone calls and a million e-mails to Congress. We helped Congress come to understand the depth of public opposition to impeachment.

(In information provided above about MoveOn was quoted directly from the organization's Web site.)

National Organization for Women (NOW)
733 15th Street NW, 2nd floor, Washington, D.C. 20005
Phone: (202) 628-8669 (628-8NOW)
Fax: (202) 785-8576
TTY: (202) 331-9002
E-mail: now@now.org
Website: http://www.now.org
(In any e-mail message, please also include a postal address and phone number since many of NOW's materials are not available through e-mail.)

The National Organization for Women works to eliminate sexism and all forms of oppression by making systemic changes in legal, political, social and economic institutions.

Founded in 1966, its first president was Betty Friedan, author of *The Feminine Mystique*. Today, NOW is the largest organization of feminist activists in the United States, with 500,000 contributing members and 550 chapters in all fifty states and the District of Columbia.

NOW's official priorities are attaining economic equality for women; supporting reproductive freedom and other women's health issues; championing civil rights; opposing racism; stopping bigotry based on sexual orientation; eliminating violence against women; and advocating for an amendment to the U.S. Constitution that will guarantee equal rights for women.

NOW's tactics include intensive lobbying, grassroots political organizing, and litigation (including class-action lawsuits). The organization also orchestrates mass marches, rallies, pickets, counter demonstrations, non-violent civil disobedience, and e-mail actions.

(This information about NOW was obtained from the organization's Web site at www.now.org.)

Women's International League for Peace and Freedom (WILPF)

1213 Race Street
Philadelphia, PA 19107-1601
Phone: (215) 563-7110
Fax: (215) 563-5527
Website: www.wilpf.org

The Women's International League for Peace and Freedom was founded in 1915 during World War I. Jane Addams was the organization's first president. During its history, the WILPF has worked towards the goals of world disarmament, full rights for women, racial and economic justice, and the elimination of all forms of violence. WILPF strives to create an environment of political, economic, social, and psychological freedom for all members of the human community so that true peace can be enjoyed by all. In today's world, WILPF works for: the equality of all people in a world free of sexism, racism, classism, and homophobia; the guarantee of fundamental human rights including the right to sustainable development; an end to all forms of violence including rape, battering, exploitation, intervention and war; the transfer of world resources from military to human needs, leading to economic justice within and among nations; and world disarmament and peaceful resolution of international conflicts via the United Nations.

(This information about the WILPF was obtained from the organization's Web site at www.wilpf.org.)

League of Women Voters

1730 M Street NW, Suite 1000, Washington, DC 20036-4508
Phone: (202) 429-1965 Fax: (202) 429-0854
E-mail: lwv@lwv.org
Website: www.lwv.org

According to its mission statement, the League of Women Voters encourages the informed and active participation of citizens in government, works to increase understanding of major public policy issues, and influences public policy through education and advocacy.

The League of Women Voters, a nonpartisan organization, has its roots in the suffragist movement of the early twentieth century. Founded only six months before the 19th amendment to the U.S. Constitution was ratified in 1920, the League has always been an activist, grassroots organization whose leaders believed that citizens should play a critical role in advocacy.

Today, the League is influential at the national, state, and local levels of government. The League's work is based on the belief that citizens who have well-researched and unbiased information will make wise decisions for their communities and their nation. The League helps citizens ensure that their voices are heard at the local, state, and national levels through coalition building around shared issues.

The League's goals for the twenty-first century include a renewed commitment to reconnecting citizens with government, enhancing voter participation, including all voices in civic life, and strengthening the democratic process through reform. More specifically, achievement of these goals involves campaign finance reform, civic education and knowledge, diversity of representation, and congressional voting representation for the District of Columbia.

(This information about the League of Women Voters was obtained from the organization's Web site at www.lwv.org.)

National Women's Political Caucus

1634 Eye Street, NW, Suite 310 Washington, DC 20006 Phone: (202) 785-1100 Fax: (202) 785-3605 E-mail: info@nwpc.org
Website: www.nwpc.org

Formed in 1971, the National Women's Political Caucus works to increase the number of women participating in political life. As a multicultural, intergenerational, and multi issue grassroots organization, the Caucus strives to create a true women's political power base that will achieve equality for all women. Such equality includes reproductive freedom, quality dependent care, and the elimination of racism, ageism, ableism, violence, poverty, and discrimination on the basis of religion or sexual orientation.

NWPC recruits, trains, and supports pro-choice women candidates for elected and appointed offices at all levels of government, regardless of party affiliation. This support includes financial donations, campaign training for candidates and campaign managers, and technical assistance and advice. State and local chapters provide support to candidates running for all levels of office by helping raise money and providing vitally important hands-on volunteer assistance. Membership in the NWPC is open to anyone who supports the goals of the organization, without regard to ethnicity, sex, nationality, age, disability, economic status, or sexual orientation.

(This information about the National Women's Political Caucus was obtained from the organization's Web site at www.nwpc.org.)

National Women's Party (NWP)

The National Women's Party NWP was founded in 1913 by Alice Paul, Lucy Burns, Crystal Eastman, and others, originally under the name Congressional Union (CU). The organization's mission was to add an amendment to the U.S. Constitution that would guarantee women the right to vote. At the time of its founding, the leading women's suffrage group, the National American Women's Suffrage Association, was working mainly on only the state level and was therefore lobbying individual states to allow women the right to vote. Thus, when the NWP formed with the intent to create a federal constitutional amendment, NAWSA felt that the members of the NWP were moving in a radical direction and ousted the group almost immediately upon its formation.

Between the time of the NWP's formation and the passage of the Nineteenth Amendment in 1920, the organization indefatigably pushed for a constitutional amendment that would guarantee women's suffrage. Even the outbreak World War I did not distract the party from its advocacy of women's suffrage. During the war, suffragists demonstrated in front of the White House with signs demanding that "Kaiser Wilson" extend democracy to women. To these brave women, it was hypocritical that President Wilson was championing democracy while

222 OUT OF THE SHADOWS

simultaneously denying suffrage to more than half the population (women and racial minorities). The NWP's non-violent, yet nonetheless blunt and aggressive, demonstrations resulted in the arrest and imprisonment of Alice Paul and other suffragists. Behind bars, however, Alice Paul and her comrades continued their protest through a prison hunger strike.

With the ratification of the Nineteenth Amendment in 1920, Alice Paul was acutely aware there was still much more to be done to achieve women's equality. In 1922, she wrote the first version of the Equal Rights Amendment, also known as the Lucretia Mott amendment. The next year, the NWP proposed the amendment as a way of eliminating sexual discrimination. Fifty years later, a new generation of feminists had built support for the amendment, and it passed both houses of Congress. Unfortunately, three fourths of the states failed to ratify the amendment by the 1982 deadline. Nevertheless, the NWP was a powerful agent of social change that helped plant the seeds of women's liberation movement.

(The information in this section on the National Women's Party was obtained and paraphrased from the Web site: http://memory.loc.gov/ammem/today/jan11.html.)

Pacifica and KPFK

KPFK 90.7 FM, Los Angeles, CA
KPFK 98.7 FM, Santa Barbara, CA
KPFK 94.1 FM, Berkeley, CA
KPFT 90.1 FM, Houston, TX
WPFW 89.3 FM, Washington, D.C.
WBAI 99.5 FM, New York, NY
http://www.kpfk.org/
http://www.pacifica.org/

Pacifica and KPFK are a listener founded radio stations that were born in the late 1940s out of the (now nearly forgotten) peace movement surrounding World War II. This era was a time when the idea of a listener sponsored radio station was a new one that had never been implemented. Nevertheless, Pacifica was born, and in 1949 KPFA went on the air from Berkeley, California.

KPFK, in Los Angeles, was the second of what would eventually become five Pacifica Stations to go on the air. Blessed with an enormous transmitter in a prime location, KPFK is the most powerful of the Pacifica stations and indeed is the most powerful public radio station in the western United States.

Pacifica's and KPFK's mission includes: contributing to a lasting understanding between nations and between the individuals of all nations, races, creeds and colors; gathering and disseminating information on the causes of conflict between any and all of such groups; and promoting the study of political and economic problems and of the causes of religious, philosophical and racial antagonisms.

(The information provided above about Pacifica and KPFK were quoted and paraphrased from the radio stations' Web sites.)

Ms. *magazine*

Phone: 1-866-MS-and-ME
E-mail:
memberservices@msmagazine.com
info@msmagazine.com
Website: http://www.msmagazine.com/index.asp

Ms. magazine is a landmark institution in both women's rights and American journalism. The founders of *Ms.*, such as Betty Friedman, have helped to shape contemporary American feminism.

Ms. was a brazen act of independence in the 1970s. At the time, the fledgling feminist movement was either denigrated or dismissed in the mainstream media, if it was mentioned at all. Most magazines for women were limited to advice about saving marriages, raising babies, or using the right cosmetics.

Soon after the first regular issue of *Ms.* hit the newsstands in July 1972, it was clear that the magazine had struck a chord with women. Its 300,000 "one-shot" test copies sold out nationwide in eight days. It generated an astonishing 26,000 subscription orders and over 20,000 reader letters within weeks.

Ms. was the first U.S. magazine to feature prominent American women demanding the repeal of laws that criminalized abortion; to explain and advocate for the ERA; to rate presidential candidates on women's issues; to put domestic violence and sexual harassment on the cover of a women's magazine; to feature feminist protest of pornography; to commission and feature a national study on date rape; and to blow the whistle on the undue influence of advertising on magazine journalism. *Ms.* was the first national magazine to make feminist voices audible, feminist journalism tenable, and a feminist world view available to the public.

Today, *Ms.* remains an interactive enterprise in which an unusually diverse readership is simultaneously engaged with each other and the world. The modern *Ms.* also boasts the most extensive coverage of international women's issues of any magazine available in the United States.

(The information provided above about *Ms.* was obtained, quoted, and paraphrased from the magazine's Web site.)

Mother Jones Magazine

731 Market Street, 6th Floor, San Francisco, CA 94103
Phone: (415) 665-6637 Fax: (415) 665-6696
E-mail: backtalk@motherjones.com
Website: http://www.motherjones.com/

Mother Jones is an independent nonprofit whose roots lie in a commitment to social justice implemented through first rate investigative reporting. Mother Jones Magazine produces revelatory journalism that in its power and reach seeks to inform and inspire a more just and democratic world

Mother Jones Magazine and Motherjones.com are made possible, in large part, by the support of the Foundation for National Progress and through donations from individual readers.

(The information provided above about Mother Jones Magazine was quoted and paraphrased from the magazine's Web site.)

The Nation magazine

33 Irving Place
New York, NY 10003
Phone: (212) 209–5400
Fax: (212) 982–9000
Website: http://www.thenation.com/

The Nation magazine has been providing unconventional wisdom since 1865. Each edition is a compilation of news and analysis on politics and culture from the left.

According to The Nation's founding prospectus, written in 1865:

The Nation will not be the organ of any party, sect, or body. It will, on the contrary, make an earnest effort to bring to the discussion of political and social questions a really critical spirit, and to wage war upon the vices of violence, exaggeration, and misrepresentation by which so much of the political writing of the day is marred.

(The information provided above about The Nation was obtained, quoted and paraphrased from the magazine's Web site.)

BIBLIOGRAPHY

The following bibliography lists the sources used to compose this book. We, the creators of this book, are indebted to the scholars, writers, activists, and other champions of human rights who have published their research and enabled us to compile their information into this book.

(Note: Additional sources, such as those on the Internet, are also listed at the end of individual chapters.)

Jane Addams, quoted in Carol Hymowitz and Michaele Weissman, A History of Women in America, Bantam Books, New York, 1978

Vera Alsop, quoted by Huw Beynon and Terry Austrin in *Masters and Servants: Class and Patronage in the Making of a Labour Organization*, Rivers Oram Press, London, 1994

Margaret Anderson, quoted in Richard Drinnon, *Rebel in Paradise: A Biography of Emma Goldman*, University of Chicago Press, Chicago, 1961

Quoted in Rosalyn Baxandall and Linda Gordon (eds.), with Susan Reverby, *America's Working Women: A Documentary History, 1600 to the Present*, W.W. Norton, New York, 1995

Lloyd George, quoted in Sarah Boston, *Women Workers and the Trade Unions*, Lawrence and Wishart, London, 1980

Teresa Billington-Greig, quoted in *Luck Bland, Banish the Beast: English Feminism and Sexual Morality*, 1885–1914, Penguin Books, Harmondsworth, 1995

Dorothy Dunbar Bromley, quoted in Glenda Riley, Inventing the American Woman: A Perspective on Women's History, 1865 to the Present, Harlan Davidson Inc., Arlingotn Hieghts, Illinois, 1986

Sarah L. and A. Elizabeth Delany, with Amy Hill Hearth, *Having Our Say: The Delany Sisters' First 100 Years*, A Dell book, Bantam Doubleday Dell Publishing Group Inc., New York, 1994

Ellen Carol DuBois, Harriot Stanton Blatch and the Transformation of Class Relations among Woman Suffragists, in Noralee Frankel and Nancy S. Dye (eds.), *Gender, Class, Race and Reform in the Progressive Era*, University Press of Kentucky, Lexington, 1991

Linda Lear, *Rachel Carson: Witness for Nature*, Henry Holt And Company, New York, 1997

Crystal Eastman, *Now We Can Begin*, in Blanche Wiesen Cook (ed.), Crystal Eastman: *On Women and Revolution*, Oxford University Press, Oxford, 1978

Crystal Eastman, quoted in Blanche Wiesen Cook (ed.), Crystal Eastman: *On Women and Revolution*, Oxford University Press, Oxford, 1978

Elizabeth Ewen, *Immigrant Women in the Land of Collars: Life and Culture on the Lower East Side*, 1890–1925, Monthly Review Press, New York, 1985

The Feminist Chronicles of the 20th Century

Dana Frank, *Purchasing Power, Consumer Organizing, Gender, and the Seattle Labor Movement, 1919–1929*, Cambridge University Press, Cambridge, 1995

Elizabeth Gurley Flynn, "Women in Industry Should Organize," in Rosalyn Fraad Baxandall, *Words on Fire: The Life and Writing of Elizabeth Gurley Flynn*, Rutgers University Press, New Brunswick, 1987

Charlotte Perkins Gilman quoted in Dolores Hayden, *The Grand Domestic Revolution*, MIT Press, Cambridge, Mass., 1984

Charlotte Perkins Gilman, Herland: *A Lost Feminist Utopian Novel*, with an introduction by Ann J. Lane, Pantheon Books, New York, 1979 (first edition 1915)

Linda Gordon, *Woman's Body, Woman's Right: A Social History of Birth Control in America*, Grossman, Viking Press, New York, 1976

Mattie Mae Halford, quoted in Philip S. Foner, *Women and the American Labor Movement: From the First Trade Unions to the Present*, The Free Press, Macmillan, New York, 1979

Arthur Hall, "The Increasing Use of Lead as an Abortifacient," British Medical Journal, 18 March 1905

Sandra Holton, *Feminism and Democracy*, Cambridge University Press, Cambridge, 1986

Mrs. Layton, "Memories of Seventy Years," in Margaret Llewellyn Davies (ed.), *Life As We Have Known It*, by Cooperative Working Women, Hogarth Press, London, 1931

Florence Luscomb, quoted in Ellen Canarow (ed.), *Moving the Mountain: Women Working for Social Change*, The Feminist Press and McGraw-Hill, New York, 1980

Aileen S. Kraditor, *The Ideas of the Woman Suffrage Movement*, 1890–1920, W.W. Norton and Co., New York, 1981

James R. McGovern, "The American Woman's Pre-World War I Freedom in Manners and Morals," Journal of American History, Vol. IV, No. 2, September 1968

Margaret Dreier Robins, quoted in Philip S. Foner, *Women and the American Labor Movement*

Alice Paul, quoted in Rosalind Rosenberg, *Divided Lives: American Women in the Twentieth Century*, Penguin Books, Harmondsworth, 1993

Dora Russell, "The Long Campaign", New Humanist, December 1974

Margaret Sanger, quoted in Linda Gordon, *Woman's Body, Woman's Right: A Social History of Birth Control in America*, Grossman, Viking Press, New York, 1976

Dorothy Sterling, *Black Foremothers: Three Lives*, The Feminist Press, New York, 1988

Anna Louise Strong, *I Change Worlds: The Remaking of an American*, Seal Press, Seattle, 1979 (first edition 1935)

Lillian Wald, "Suffrage 1914," in Clare Coss (ed.), Lillian D. Wald, Progressive Activist, The Feminist Press, New York, 1989

Melvina Walker, "My Impression of the Women's Conference", *The Workers' Dreadnought*, 2 November 1918

Barbara Woloch, *Women and the American Experience: A Concise History*, Overture Books, The McGraw-Hill Companies Inc., New York, 1996

Virginia Woolf, "A Room of One's Own," in Virginia Woolf, *A Room of One's Own and Three Guineas*, with an introduction by Hermione Lee, Chatto and Windus, Hogarth Press, London, 1984

Virginia Woolf, quoted in Judith Hattaway, Virginia Woolf's Jacob's Room, History and Memory, in Dorothy Goldman (ed.), *Women and World War I: The Written Response*, Macmillan, London, 1993